1

AUTO-AVIO COSTRUZIONI

Enzo Ferrari                                    Modena-Italia

Viale Trento Trieste 11 - Telefono 4061 - Casella Postale 222 - U.P.C. 3566 - Telegrafo: Enzo Ferrari

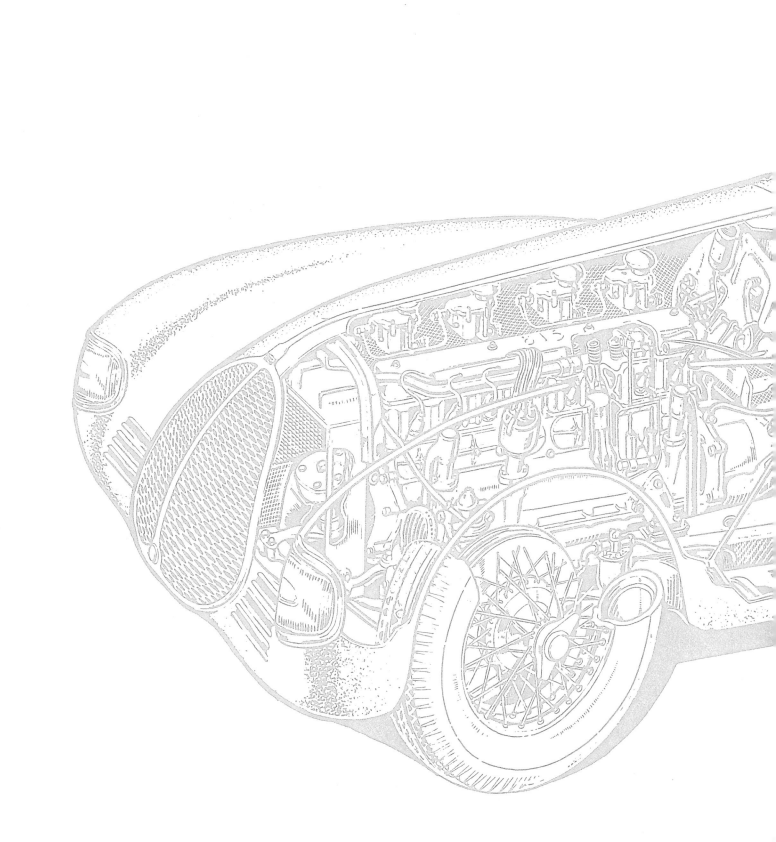

FRANCO VARISCO

# 815

# THE GENESIS OF FERRARI

WORLD

# CONTENTS

# PREFACE

THREE SIMPLE NUMBERS, 815. APPARENTLY UNDRAMATIC AND UNINSPIRING. YET, OVER 50 YEARS AGO, THESE NUMBERS SIGNALLED THE BEGINNING OF THE GREATEST LEGEND IN AUTOMOTIVE HISTORY, THEY COMPRISED THE NAME OF THE FIRST CARS BUILT BY ENZO FERRARI.

HIS DISAGREEMENTS WITH UGO GOBBATO, THE HEAD OF ALFA ROMEO, CULMINATED IN HIM LEAVING THE COMPANY IN 1939.

THE MAN FROM MODENA LEFT AS DIRECTOR OF ALFA RACING WITH A LARGE SUN OF MONEY, SIGNED AN AGREEMENT NOT TO REBUILD THE SCUDERIA FERRARI FOR A PERIOD OF AT LEAST FOUR YEARS AND ALSO NOT TO WORK IN THE RACING BUSINESS. QUALIFIED INDEPENDENCE FOR ENZO FERRARI WAS THE RESULT, AND HENCE THE PRANCING HORSE WAS LET LOOSE. FERRARI FOUNDED HIS FIRM OF AUTO AVIO COSTRUZIONI IN MODENA BUT LATER IN 1943 IT FOUND ITS PERMANENT HOME AT MARANELLO. HE BUILT COMPONENTS FOR SMALL 4-CYLINDER ENGINES FOR TRAINING AIRCRAFT AND THEN HYDRAULIC GRINDERS FOR THE PRODUCTION OF BALL-BEARINGS.

BUT FERRARI WAS A MAN WHO THOUGHT ABOUT MOTOR RACING DAY AND NIGHT. DESPITE THE OUTBREAK OF THE SECOND WORLD WAR, BRESCIA DID NOT CANCEL THE MILLE MIGLIA RACE IN 1940, PERHAPS FOR POLITICAL REASONS ALTHOUGH THE ORGANISERS ABANDONED THE TRADITIONAL COURSE OF BRESCIA-ROMA-BRESCIA. THE LEGENDARY LONG-DISTANCE RACE, UNIQUE IN THE HISTORY OF THE AUTOMOBILE, WAS TO BE RUN ON THE TRIANGLE RUNNING FROM BRESCIA-CREMONA-MANTUA-BRESCIA: A VERY LONG STRAIGHT LINE WITH CURVES AT THE CORNERS OF THE TRIANGLE - NO CLIMBS, NO DESCENTS, STRAIGHT LINES ALL THE WAY.

FERRARI SET OFF ON HIS OWN TRACK AND CREATED THE 815 - THREE FIGURES WHICH HAD THE SWEET SCENT OF REVENGE. 815: THEY WERE THE SAME NUMBERS, EVEN IF REARRANGED, OF THE 158 (1500 CC 8-CYLINDER WITH SUPERCHARGER) CREATED BY THE FERRARI SCUDERIA AT MODENA IN 1937, WHICH LATER BECAME AN ALFA ROMEO. AS THE 158, AND THEN IN MODIFIED FORM AS THE 159, THE LEGENDARY SINGLE-SEATER WAS TO WIN THE WORLD DRIVERS' CHAMPIONSHIPS OF 1950 AND 1951 WITH NINO FARINA AND JUAN MANUEL FANGIO. FERRARI TOLD

ME THAT HE RECEIVED 800,000 LIRE (AROUND £ 400) FOR THE FOUR 158'S WHICH HE SOLD TO ALFA IN 1939.

SO TO THE 815. THE PLAN WAS ALBERTO MASSIMINO'S, A MAN WHO HAD LEFT ALFA AFTER FERRARI. AT MASSIMINO'S SIDE THERE WAS VITTORIO BELLENTANI, AND THE PRESENT WRITER WAS TO ESTABLISH FRIENDLY RELATIONS WITH BOTH OF THEM, SOMEWHAT RESERVED WITH MASSIMINO BUT MUCH CLOSER WITH BELLENTANI.

IT WAS INEVITABLE THAT FERRARI WASN'T GOING TO USE A SINGLE SCREW FROM ALFA. THE CAR WAS LARGELY MADE UP OF FIAT MATERIALS. THE 8 CYLINDER, 1,500 CC CONFIGURATION BELONGED TO NO-ONE, THOUGH, AND FERRARI KNEW IT WORKED FROM HIS EXPERIENCE WITH THE ALFA 158.

FERRARI, AS USUAL, WAS IN A HURRY. THE ENGINE WAS THE RESULT OF COMBINING TWO FIAT 1100S WHOSE CAPACITY HAD BEEN REDUCED. (FERRARI HAD NEVER SAID MUCH ABOUT THE DETAILS OF HIS PROTOTYPE.) THE SPYDER COACHWORK WAS BY TOURING OF MILAN AND THEREFORE SPLENDID. IN A FEW MONTHS THE TWO 815'S WERE READY. THEY DIDN'T BEAR THE MAKER'S NAME - FOLLOWING THE AGREEMENT WITH ALFA - BUT FERRARI KNEW WITH OBSTINATE CERTAINTY THAT, WITH THE END OF THE WAR, CARS WOULD EMERGE WHICH WOULD BE TOTALLY HIS. IT JUST NEEDED THE ARRIVAL OF PEACE. THEN HE WOULD SEE ...

TO WHOM SHOULD HE ENTRUST THE TWO 815S? THE DECISION DIDN'T TAKE LONG: ONE WOULD BE FOR ALBERTO ASCARI, THE 22-YEAR OLD ORPHANED SON OF THE GREAT CHAMPION ANTONIO WHO HAD BEEN AT ALFA IN THE TWENTIES WITH FERRARI; THE OTHER WAS TO BE FOR THE MARCHESE LOTARIO RANGONI MACHIAVELLI OF MODENA.

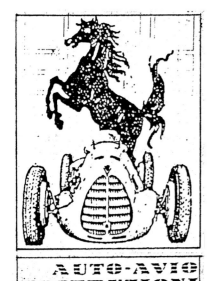

ALBERTO ASCARI HAD ALREADY RACED MOTORCYCLES, PERHAPS CARS TOO. HE HAD A VERY LIVELY DRIVER'S TEMPERAMENT, WAS NEVER ABLE TO TAKE HIS FOOT OFF THE ACCELERATOR AND HAD LITTLE RESPECT FOR THE CAR. WHAT COUNTED WAS GOING FAST. SO FERRARI PUT HIM BESIDE SOMEONE WHO COULD HOLD HIM BACK A BIT, GIOVANNI MINOZZI, THE SON OF MARIANNA, ANTONIO ASCARI'S SISTER. WITH RANGONI MACHIAVELLI THERE WAS ENRICO NARDI, A REAL MASTER OF MECHANICS. HE WAS A DRIVER TOO, LATER A BUILDER WHO IN 1947 FOUNDED A COMPANY MANUFACTURING SPORTS CARS AT TURIN WITH RENATO DANESE. LATER NARDI WAS TO BECOME FAMOUS FOR HIS STEERING WHEELS, WHICH WOULD BE FITTED TO FERRARIS AND SOME OF THE OTHER MOST PRESTIGIOUS CARS IN THE WORLD.

ON 28 APRIL 1940 THE AUTHOR WAS ON THE STRAIGHT STRETCH JOINING THE BRESCIA-CREMONA CORNER TO CREMONA-MANTUA. FOR THE CURVE COMING FROM BRESCIA THEY HAD SPECIALLY CONSTRUCTED A 'PARABOLICA' (BANKING), NOT VERY STEEP (IT STILL EXISTS TODAY), WHICH CREATED A LOT OF ENTHUSIASM FOR THE GODDESS OF SPEED. THE OTHER CURVE TOWARDS MANTUA, ALSO NEW, WAS COMPLETELY FLAT.

I REMEMBER THAT IN THE DAYS PRIOR TO THE RACE MY DEAR CHEMISTRY TEACHER, RUSCONI, BETWEEN ONE LESSON AND ANOTHER USED TO SAY CONTINUALLY "LET'S HOPE THEY DON'T WIN!"- "THEY" WERE THE GERMAN BMW CREW WHO ACTUALLY DOMINATED THE ALFAS AND WON THE RACE. ON THE FOLLOWING MONDAY, RUSCONI WAS FURIOUS AND SPOKE TO US AT GREAT LENGTH, FEARLESSLY, ABOUT WHAT WAS GOING

TO HAPPEN TO THE WORLD. HE WAS RIGHT IN EVERY RESPECT. DEAR PROFESSOR, WITH THAT BEAUTIFUL WHITE BULL-DOG OF YOURS, AS WELL-BEHAVED AS ITS OWNER, A GENTLEMAN IN THE ENGLISH TRADITION.

FRANCO VARISCO TOLD ME, BEFORE I WROTE THESE LINES, THAT FERRARI WAS PRESENT DURING PRACTICE AND THE RACE ITSELF AT THE 'PARABOLICA'. WHO WOULD EVER HAVE IMAGINED THAT I, AT THAT TENDER AGE, WAS SO CLOSE TO THE MAN WHO AFFECTED MY LIFE SO MUCH - AND STILL DOES? I REMEMBER THE TWO 815S WELL. IN PADANIA AND ESPECIALLY IN CREMONA, PEOPLE KNEW WHO ENZO FERRARI WAS, THROUGH THE MANY FRIENDS HE MADE IN THE MOTORING WORLD. LET'S GO BACK TO 1940. THE TRIANGLE WAS 165 KILOMETRES LONG AND HAD TO BE LAPPED NINE TIMES, EQUIVALENT TO 1,485 km. AT THE END OF THE FIRST LAP, ASCARI-MINOZZI WERE LYING 12TH AND RANGONI MACHIAVELLI-NARDI WERE 13TH. IN THE SECOND LAP, ASCARI HAD TO RETIRE WHILE THE OTHER 815 CARRIED ON BRILLIANTLY. ON THE SEVENTH LAP RANGONI-NARDI WERE TENTH, BUT DURING THE NEXT LAP THEY TOO HAD TO DROP OUT.

IN THE MAGAZINE 'AUTO ITALIANA', GIOVANNI LURANI, A GOOD DRIVER AND JOURNALIST WROTE: "IN THE 1,500CC CLASS, THE INITIATION OF THE 815 WAS EXCITING AND CONVINCING. IT IS NO MEAN ACHIEVEMENT, KNOWING HOW TO DESIGN FROM SCRATCH AND PRESENT TWO HIGH-QUALITY SPORTS CARS IN ONLY FOUR MONTHS, WHICH IN THE SEVEREST AND FASTEST RACE IN THE WORLD DARED TO DOMINATE THE FIELD WITH THE GREATEST OF EASE FOR NINE-TENTHS OF THE COMPETITION, HAVING TO GIVE UP ONLY BECAUSE OF THOSE INEVITABLE SMALL FAULTS TO BE FOUND IN ANY NEW CONSTRUCTION. THEY WERE CERTAINLY NOT DUE TO THE DESIGN, WHICH WAS SOUND IN BOTH CONCEPT AND REALISATION. THE 174 KM/H MOST OFTEN CLOCKED DURING THE RACE TELLS US THAT THE 815'S WERE ALREADY, FROM THE MOMENT THEY FIRST CAME OUT, THE FASTEST CARS IN THEIR CLASS IN CIRCULATION."

SO, THE 'ANTEPRIMA' HAD ALREADY ANNOUNCED HOW MUCH THE MAN FROM MODENA WANTED TO BE KNOWN. BUT WHERE DID THE TWO 815'S END UP? FERRARI NEVER SPOKE TO ME ABOUT THEM. FOR HIM, ONCE THE RACE WAS FINISHED, THE CAR WAS DEAD, GONE WITH THE WIND. AND PERHAPS IT NEVER CROSSED HIS MIND THAT ONE OF THEM COULD HAVE BEEN SAVED. YEARS LATER HE WAS TO SAY TO ME: "I NEVER KEPT ANYTHING BECAUSE I COULDN'T ALLOW MYSELF. I HAD TO GET BACK WHAT WAS LEFT TO USE IN OTHER MACHINES. AND YOU TALK OF A MUSEUM: BUT WHAT MUSEUM WAS I SUPPOSED TO MAKE? I COULDN'T, AND THAT'S ALL THERE IS TO IT."

IF THERE WERE STILL AN 815, WHO KNOWS WHERE, I WOULD BE HAPPY JUST TO LOOK AT IT AND STROKE IT. JUST AS I WOULD HAVE DONE TO THE FACE OF A YOUNG LADY-FRIEND OF THE TIME WHO, BY A MAGICAL COINCIDENCE, HAD THE SURNAME FERRARI. HER NAME? THAT'S A SECRET.

GINO RANCATI

10       *From this letter we can get an idea of the plan Ferrari was hatching for the contruction of a new racing-car.*

# FERRARI FOUNDS AUTO AVIO COSTRUZIONI AT MODENA

**ENZO FERRARI - MODENA**

| R | EF | dir. |
|---|----|------|

Modena 6. Novembre 1939XVIII
Viale Trento Trieste N. II - C.P.E. N° 35644
Telefono 4081 - Telegrammi: Enzo Ferrari - Modena

Ill.mo Signor
Comm. CASTAGNETO
Direttore del R.A.C.I.
Piazza della Vittoria n.7
B R E S C I A

Caro Castagneto,

ho ricevuto il ritaglio del "Popolo di Brescia" che segue
l'annuncio del Comunicato F.A.S.I.

La "Mille Miglia" è dunque entrata in cantiere per una nuo=
va superba edizione ?

Ne ero sicuro, e tanto che, passando da Modena, potrete con=
statare sino a qual punto io ne sia convinto....!

Molti cordiali saluti.

1939. Certainly not a happy year. A great part of Europe was already at war and Italy was about to be involved as well. Enzo Ferrari was 41 years old and by then had been involved in racing cars for 22 of them: as a driver from 1919 to 1932, then as founder and driving-spirit of the 'Scuderia' of the same name from 1929 to 1935 and finally as director of the 'Alfa Corse' from 1936 to 1938. Suddenly, however, his long involvement with Alfa

Romeo came to an end, and he left for good after bitter disagreements with some of the other directors. The Milanese firm obliged him however to sign an undertaking not to rebuild the 'Scuderia Ferrari' or to engage in racing activity before four years had elapsed."

"Scuderia Ferrari was a joint-stock company," wrote Enzo Ferrari, "and as such had been liquidated. With the proceeds from that liquidation and my own from Alfa,

12

I founded Auto Avio Costruzioni at Modena." That was how Ferrari found the way to get round the obstacle, bringing to life a new company working on aero-engine components, still based in Modena at No.11, viale Trento e Trieste, in the same premises as the old 'Scuderia'. It was a small but very well equipped workshop with 45 employees ready for any sacrifice and above all skilled, fast and precise. Some days before the end of 1939, near Christmas Eve, Ferrari received a visit in his new factory from two young men in search of excitement who asked him to build a pair of racing cars to satisfy their passion. Ferrari, impetuous by nature, didn't wait to be asked a second time, and as he had always done, took an immediate decision to build a new racing car. Consequently a real miracle was performed. In little more than two months the new car was off the drawing-board and on the road, and after another month of testing two models were ready to make their debut in the first

*Milan, 1940.*
*In this photo, autographed by Ferrari, we see the newly completed 815 by Carrozzeria Touring, in front of the entrance to the Autostrada dei Laghi, near Musocco, a little way from via Ludovico di Breme, where Touring were based.*

Brescia Grand Prix, which replaced the Mille Miglia banned by the authorities after the accidents in the 1938 race.

The new car wasn't called Ferrari because, of course its inventor could not put his own name to any car. In fact the name Ferrari never appeared on any part of the car: neither on the body nor the engine, nor even on the official documents. It was called simply '815'

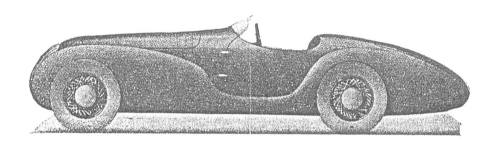

(8-cylinders, 1.5 litres) but it was certainly the first Ferrari car. Actually, the 'anteprima'. Even if it didn't find a place in the official history of the Prancing Horse, it was the first real demonstration of Ferrari as a car-maker, because on this adventure, as in so many others, Enzo Ferrari left the stamp of his great determination and his incisive personality.

14

The two examples of the 815 were built to be entered in the 'Sport Nazionale' category recently introduced by F.A.S.I. (Federazione Automobilistica Sportiva Italiana - Italian motor racing federation).

Enzo Ferrari preferred to enter the field in the up-to-1500cc class so as not to be in direct competition with the fearful BMWs in the 2-litre class or the powerful Alfa Romeos in the 3-litre class. The car from Modena therefore had to compete with much less competitive cars, such as the Lancia Aprilias and the Fiat 1500s which had special lightweight bodywork, both open and closed. When the two cars were ready Ferrari, following what was to become a habit of his, handed out slips of paper with a few lines of presentation, written in his own hand, complete with information and technical details:

*February 1940.*
*The first road trials of the 815. Enrico Nardi, drove thousands of kilometres on the roads of Emilia to get the car into shape. Standing on the kerb under the road-sign, a significant spectator is Ernesto Maserati.*

**Enzo Ferrari · C.P.C. 35644 · telephone 4081 · Viale Trento e Trieste, 11, Modena**

*The following prospectus is for information only and is not binding.*

## AUTO AVIO COSTRUZIONI

## Modena · Italia 1940 · XVIII

## 8 C. 1500 cc 815

"In producing this small sports car, which we will call the 815, we have not intended to build a new car, but simply to present you with a new type which is the result of modifications to existing components, from our research and engineering. Our 20-years experience in high-performance motoring and our thorough awareness of the numerous needs that arise from the use of the high-powered car destined for sporting competition, have guided us in the production of the 815. With its highly individual characteristics which are not be found in any series production, it offers the certainty of satisfying your sporting needs. The extreme simplicity of the engine, the total interchangeability of the parts forming the chassis, the speed, the acceleration, the limited fuel consumption, the remarkably low weight and the perfect stability are the synthesis of the 815."

16

| AUTO AVIO COSTRUZIONI | | SPECIFICATIONS | |
|---|---|---|---|
| Engine with cylinders in line | 8 | Track | 124 cm |
| Total displacement | 1496cc | Independent front suspension, | |
| Bore and stroke | 63 x 60mm | rear axle with leaf-springs | |
| Peak revs per minute | 5500 | Worm and screw steering, right-hand drive. | |
| Maximum power | 72 bhp | Pedal-operated hydraulic brakes | |
| Water cooling with centrifugal pump | 1 | on all four wheels | |
| Weber carburettors | 2 (4) | Rudge-Borrani wheels type DD | 15x3.25 |
| Coil ignition | | Pirelli tyres type Stella Bianca | 5.50x15 |
| and Bosch distributors | 2 | Complete Bosch electrical system | 12 volt |
| Pressurised lubrication | | Fuel tank capacity | 108 litres |
| with geared pump | 2 | Fuel consumption per 100 km | 13 - 15 litres |
| Dry-plate clutch | 1 | Weight of chassis and spare | |
| Gears with reverse, 3rd silent, | | wheel without body | 535 kg |
| 3rd and 4th synchronised | 4 | Speed | 160-170 km/h |
| Wheelbase | 242 cm | 2-seater Torpedo-type Brescia body | |

*Milan 1940. The 815 in the square in front of the entrance to the Autostrada dei Laghi at the bottom of viale Certosa (on the North-West edge of the city); in the background a part of the 14th century Carthusian monastery of Garegnano.*

18        *The trade-mark of Auto Avio Costruzioni on the cover of the publicity brochure for the 815.*

# THE FIRST CAR,
# CREATED IN JUST A FEW WEEKS

The very limited time available to produce the car compelled Ferrari and his colleagues to use existing components as much as possible.

In the meantime Fiat, in order to demonstrate its lively interest in the first Brescia Grand Prix (the Mille Miglia), put at the disposal of the organisers three prizes of 5,000 lire for each of the three classes (750 cc, 1,100 cc and 1,500 cc) to be given to the first competitor in a Fiat-built car or with at least a Fiat chassis.

The designer took as his starting-point the Fiat 508 C, a great production car ahead of its time which for some years had enjoyed great success both with the public and with specialist convertors.

20

The chassis was suitably adapted and reinforced to take the strain of greater power, while the front and rear suspension, brakes, transmission and steering of the Fiat 508 C were all up to the standard required.

*Top: the independent front suspension. Bottom: the chassis of the 508 C.*
*Opposite page: two views of the 508 C. The designers of the new Ferrari car borrowed*
*extensively from this highly successful design.*

The most difficult problem was with the engine. It was decided to plan and construct an in-line 8-cylinder, in practice joining two Fiat 1100 engines and reducing the displacement to 1.5 litres. It was important however to use the greatest number of Fiat parts possible to gain time and reduce costs.

The cylinder block and oil sump, amply finned for cooling, were completely remade in aluminium and produced at the Calzoni Foundry in Bologna; so too was the valve cover with '815' written on it in relief. On the other hand the 5-bearing crankshaft and the

camshaft with 16 cams were built at the Ferrari workshop in Modena. Valves, valve springs, rocker arms and connecting rods were all original Fiat parts.

Two heads from the 508 C were placed in-line on the cylinder block. The pair of ignition distributors which had been difficult to synchronise were replaced by one specially made, this also activated the rev-counter. A new water-pump was installed, larger because of the increased engine capacity. Four new inverted carburettors

*The in-line 8-cylinder engine of the 815 seen from the intake side and the exhaust side. On the rocker cover can be seen in relief: 815. Note the four carburettors, Ferrari's brochure claimed two.*

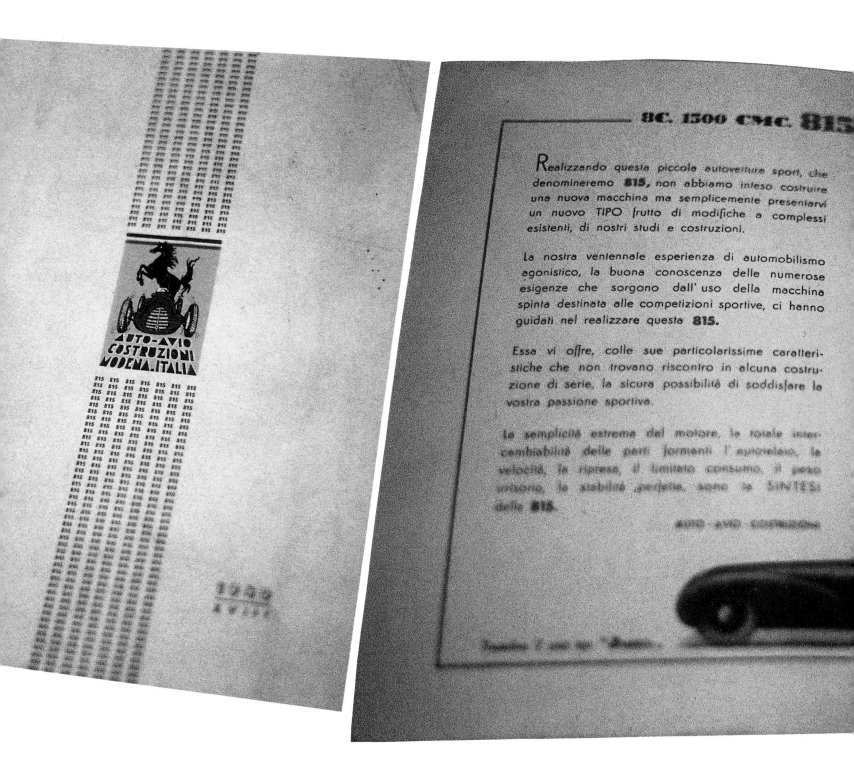

*The publicity folder produced by Enzo Ferrari to introduce his new car and detail its technical specifications.*

supplied the engine with fuel, placed between the pipes of the exhaust manifold which fed into a single pipe terminating at the rear right. The compression ratio was increased compared to the standard Fiat from 6:1 to 7:1. The bodywork for this new Sports 815, produced by Touring of Milan was distinguished by its elegance, economy, and lightness. It was made of a special aluminium-magnesium alloy called 'Itallumag 35', an unusual and costly material. For the 815, Touring had studied various solutions to find the most appropriate shape for the body.

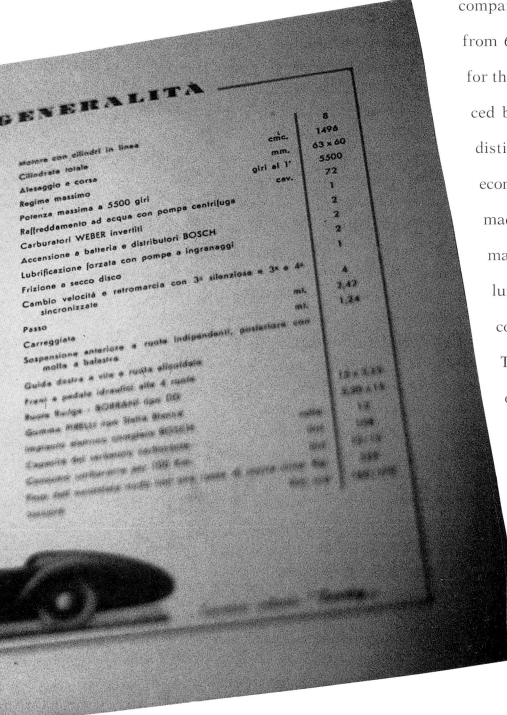

In the meantime news was out that Ferrari wanted to produce about ten examples of the 815. But the temperamental designer promptly denied it when, on 14 February 1940, the Gazzetta dello Sport published the following lines: "Enzo Ferrari is building a series of 1100 cc Sports cars" (rather than 1500) "with eight cylinders in line".

Meanwhile the first car was almost ready to be put on the road.

*Rough sketches of the 815, the steering wheel and the instrument-panel reduced to the minimum.*

# THE DESIGNERS

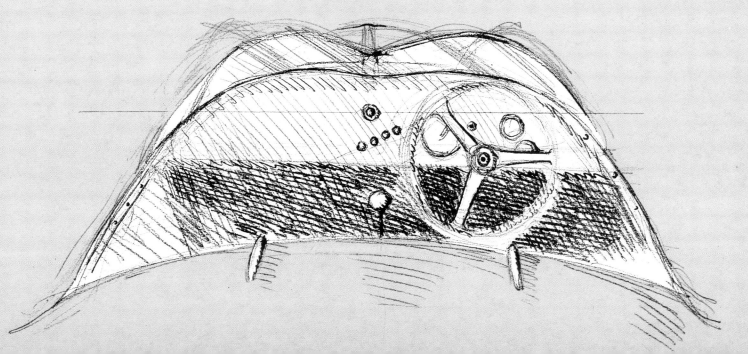

28

# ALBERTO MASSIMINO

**A**lberto Massimino was born at Turin in 1895. After graduating abroad as an engineer, he entered the specialist construction office of Fiat in 1924. In a short time he would prove himself a good designer.

In 1928, after having taken part in various interesting projects (among which the last competition car produced by the Turin company, the 12-cylinder 806) he left Fiat, where he had reached the position of Planning Manager. From 1928 to 1931 he continued his work in the aeronautical field at the aviation department of the Farina establishment; from 1931 to 1937 he was once more with Fiat, as manager of engine design.

In 1938 he moved to Modena to work with Ferrari, the director of Alfa Racing. The team, composed of Alberto Massimino and other worthy technicians like Luigi Bazzi, Gioachino Colombo and Federico Giberti, created a car destined to signal a fundamentally significant stage in the history of sports motoring: the Alfa Romeo 158, designed and produced at Modena and later sent to the parent company in Milan.

*The engineer Alberto Massimino, who played a major role in the designing of the car. It was probably he who suggested the use of Fiat components.*

Alberto Massimino remained at Modena through less glorious moments as well, such as the break with Alfa Romeo and the ban on reconstituting the Scuderia (and therefore on competing in sports events). Most importantly he was at Ferrari's side when he founded Auto Avio Costruzioni. Aided by Vittorio Bellentani he created the 815, the precursor of a whole series of famous cars.

In the production of this car Massimino decided to use numerous Fiat parts and in this way was able to take full advantage of the vast experience he had accumulated during his years in Turin.

Immediately after the war he went on to the workshops of Alfieri Maserati as manager of the technical office. In 1952 he left the marque of the Trident in order to return to Maranello as an adviser.

# VITTORIO BELLENTANI

**V**ittorio Bellentani was born at Modena on 11 November 1906 and gained a diploma in engineering in his native city. After further study at the University of Freibourg in Switzerland he began work at a factory in Modena, Guerzoni and Guarinoni, which produced Mignon motorcycles.

In 1940 Ferrari summoned him to Auto Avio Costruzioni to assist Massimino in his design work.

Thus for Bellentani began a collaboration which was to lead him to participate in the legendary 815 project, marvellously achieved in an incredibly short time to enable the car to take part in the first Mille Miglia Grand Prix at Brescia in April 1940. During the war, complying with the needs of production, he worked on the manufacture of hydraulic grinders, based on a German design, for which however Ferrari was not able to get a licence for bureaucratic reasons.

*The engineer Vittorio Bellentani with Enzo Ferrari. After contributing to the 815 project he was a faithful retainer to the Maranello company for many years.*

30

In 1949 Bellentani left Ferrari to go on to Maserati. This was, however, only a temporary separation. In fact, in 1955 Bellentani returned to Ferrari. His re-entry to Maranello coincided with a rather unfortunate time in the sport, though this was to be resolved after Lancia's donation of all their Formula 1 material. Having reached pensionable age, he continued to work for Ferrari as an external advisor until 1963. Finally, having detached himself completely from the Maranello factory, he founded a small firm in Modena which assembled the ASA, a small-engined motor car which became famous with nick-name 'Ferrarina' or 'little Ferrari'.

Superleggera
Interamente Metallica
Profilata al Vento
Brevettata

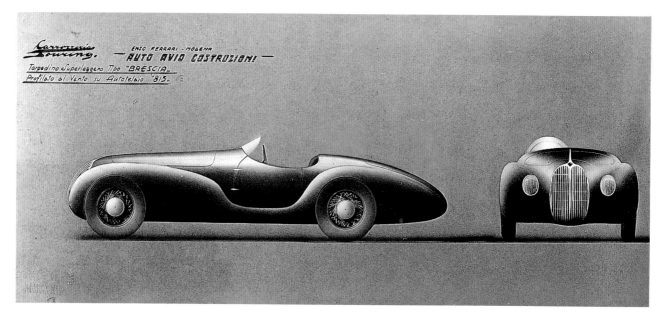

32

*Enzo Ferrari entrusted the work of 'dressing' his 815 to Carrozzeria Touring of Milan.*

Carlo Felice Bianchi Anderloni

# "WHY FERRARI
# CHOSE TOURING"

Carlo Felice Bianchi Anderloni was the second generation at Touring. Elegant, kind, cordial, enthusiastic, though his reserve, perhaps modesty, left one with the impression of a certain Calvinism, a reluctance to take the limelight, a gentlemanly aloofness in what had been 'papa's bodyshop', the celebrated Touring of Milan.

*The 815 was a very elegant, refined car, just as Enzo Ferrari wanted it. At the front near the moulded headlights, are the brake-cooling vents. To the Rear, two details worth noticing are the recessed filler-cap and the ornate light above the number plate. The Borrani wire wheels also, added a touch of class.*

"When Enzo Ferrari came to Touring in 1940," recounts Ing. Anderloni, "I was at Bra, on the officer-cadet training course for horse artillery. Papa was telling me about the man he knew from the time when Ferrari used to work at Alfa Romeo. A man, he said, with clear ideas. Speaking to my father about the 815 he suddenly came to the point: "Look, I want a car that can be recognised at a glance, that someone can look at and say: that's a Ferrari!" [even though at that time no cars with that name had been made .] "But it must also have Touring styling. Not just a racing car, something with a touch of luxury."

34

Bianchi Anderloni continues: "Ferrari was forced to use the marque name Auto Avio Costruzioni but he asked us to help him get round the problem of the name". And the line of that 815, born in the workshops at via Lodovico di Breme, shows the course of that research, with the radiator different from the brochure picture, and the stylised Prancing Horse inserted into the badge. "For the rest, Ferrari continued with his usual prudent commercial sense. He had already sold the two cars we were getting ready for him. One was for the Marchese Lotario Rangoni Machiavelli, for whom the production had to be de luxe: from the leather upholstery to details like the arrangement of the side lights or the recessed petrol cap. On the other hand, Ferrari had given the other model to the young Alberto Ascari, for about 20,000 lire, and it had to be a bit more spartan. Alberto, who lived on Corso Sempione near the bodyshop, used to drop in every so

*Superleggera*

35

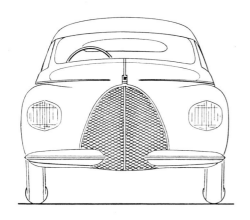

often, 'by chance'. But his curiosity, his anxiety to see the 815 completed, betrayed him. He looked, he touched, he questioned with the unmistakable passion which for him was only just beginning."

There is a photo of Ascari in his 815 when it had just come out of the bodyshop, which shows him at the wheel not far from via Lodovico di Breme in the square which leads on to the Laghi autostrada. In those days of 1940 when the winds of war were also blowing through Italy, the Mille Miglia marked the triumph of Touring, with BMW in first place and Alfa in second, both bodies made by the Milanese workshop. But that was also the debut of the 815 in the famous race. Bianchi Anderloni continues: "Ferrari was already thinking about after the war, even if Mussolini hadn't yet made a declaration of war. He was thinking about an 815 convertible, a little different from the racing type, to be marketed in better times. We also made him a little model that looked like the Alfa 2500. And that scale model, which never came to anything, I found many years later in Ferrari's house: he kept it on a dresser in Modena, like a table decoration." Touring's methods were typical of an artisan's workshop, what would have been called an artist's studio in the renaissance. "How did we work on the 815? The usual way. Papa was a creative man. Whenever he went to bed he had a pen and paper on the bed-side table. Then in the night he would wake up with a start with an idea in his head, and that idea would be furiously scribbled down by the weak light of the bedside lamp. Papa would throw down the drawing and then the 'visualisers' would come in, like Formenti, and realise the idea." Cars designed by Touring, were said to be

*Technical drawing from Touring based on the Auto Avio Costruzioni chassis, drawn in pencil and indian ink on tracing paper.*
*A small number of these of these elegant convertibles were to have been produced, but the plan was dropped with the advent of the war. The photograph is the first of Alberto Ascari at the wheel of the 815, a short way from Carrozzeria Touring.*

36

'drawn in the wind' and the same could be said of the 815. We carried the 1/10th scale model to the wind tunnel, or 'aerodynamic conduit' as it used to be called at the time, from Breda at Bresso. But the refining tests were always done live, on the road. Once it was finished, threads of wool were stuck to the bodywork of the 815 and it was taken out on to the autostrada. We had two places to try it out: the Milan-Bergamo road or the Milan-Como one. The 815 ended up in the region of the lakes. After the Como-Varese turn-off, going towards Lainate, there was a long flattish stretch. It was an ideal run, which Jano had 'discovered' when he was with Alfa Romeo for meas-

uring maximum speed. The 815 was also launched several times along that road which was almost always deserted, and we tried to stay behind or to get alongside her in another car with the photographer on board. The poor chap had to lean out into the wind, with his bellows-camera, in order to capture on film the behaviour of the flowing woollen threads, those aerodynamic spies. That shape designed by the air was our secret. And papa's motto for Touring also held good for the 815: "Weight is the enemy, and wind resistance the obstacle."

38 *The cover of the regulations issued by the organisers for the First Gran Premio Brescia delle Mille Miglia.*

COMITATO OLIMPICO NAZIONALE ITALIANO

## FEDERAZIONE AUTOMOBILISTICA SPORTIVA ITALIANA

C O N I

# REALE AUTOMOBILE CIRCOLO D'ITALIA

SEDE PROVINCIALE DI BRESCIA

# 1° GRAN PREMIO BRESCIA

DELLE

# MILLE MIGLIA

## 28 APRILE 1940-XVIII

## *Regolamento*

# 1° GRAN PREMIO BRESCIA
## DELLE "MILLE MIGLIA"
### 28 APRILE 1940 · XVIII

## IL PERCORSO

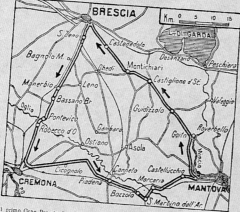

Il primo Gran Premio Brescia delle "Mille Miglia" si snoda attraverso le Province di BRESCIA - CREMONA e MANTOVA.
Sui veloci rettilinei della Statale 45 bis si toccano: S. Zeno - Bagnolo Mella - Manerbio Pontevico - Olmeneta e si giunge a Cremona dopo aver percorso Km. 48. Lasciata la città del Torrazzo si entra nella statale n. 10. Un lungo rettilineo fino a Piadena che si attraversa, e si entra nella provincia di Mantova. Poi Bozzolo, Marcaria, Castellucchio (Km. 104). A Castellucchio il percorso devia per la comunale Grazie Goito passante per Rivalta e Sacca, e che si innesta a Goito nella provinciale Mantova - Brescia (Km. 119). Guidizzolo - Castiglione delle Stiviere, Montichiari e Castenedolo vengono toccati prima che a Brescia l'anello si ricongiunga. Il percorso è di circa 165 Km. da ripetersi nove volte per totali Km. 1485 circa.

---

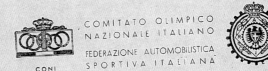

COMITATO OLIMPICO
NAZIONALE ITALIANO
FEDERAZIONE AUTOMOBILISTICA
SPORTIVA ITALIANA
CONI

# 1° GRAN PREMIO BRESCIA
## DELLE «MILLE MIGLIA»

Manifestazione internazionale aperta di velocità indetta in conformità del Codice Sportivo Internazionale, del Regolamento Nazionale Sportivo ed annesso Regolamento Nazionale per vetture Sport; valida per la classifica del Campionato Italiano Categoria Sport.

### 28 Aprile 1940 - XVIII

## Regolamento

---

# REGOLAMENTO

**DEFINIZIONI e LIMITI**

Art. 1 - Il Reale Automobile Circolo d'Italia, Sede Provinciale di Brescia, a mezzo di uno speciale Comitato appositamente costituito, e con la collaborazione delle Sedi del R. A. C. I. di Cremona e di Mantova, indice ed organizza per il giorno 28 Aprile 1940 - XVIII una manifestazione internazionale aperta di velocità denominata:

### I. GRAN PREMIO BRESCIA DELLE «MILLE MIGLIA»

Art. 2 - La manifestazione è valida per la classifica del Campionato Italiano della categoria Sport Nazionale per l'anno 1940 - XVIII.

Art. 3 - Il presente regolamento è redatto e la manifestazione è organizzata in conformità al Regolamento Nazionale Sportivo della F.A.S.I. ed annesso regolamento per Vetture Sport, ed al Codice Sportivo Internazionale dell'A. I. A. C. R. e relativi annessi.

**PERCORSO**

Art. 4 - La corsa sarà disputata sul seguente percorso chiuso al traffico:
BRESCIA - Manerbio - CREMONA - Piadena - Bozzolo - Castellucchio - Grazie - Goito - Castiglione Montichiari - BRESCIA, dello sviluppo di Km. 165, da ripetersi nove volte per totali Km. 1485 circa.

3

---

**VETTURE AMMESSE**

Art. 5 - Alla manifestazione saranno ammesse le vetture italiane comprese nell'Elenco delle vetture Sport Nazionali redatto dalla F.A.S.I., e le vetture di costruzione estera, rispondenti ai requisiti prescritti dal Regolamento Nazionale per Vetture Sport. Qualsiasi tipo di vettura (nazionale o straniera) dovrà presentare tutti gli elementi fondamentali inalterabili enumerati dal predetto Regolamento.

I concorrenti italiani o stranieri che intendono iscrivere una vettura di marca estera dovranno trasmettere una dichiarazione firmata attestante che le caratteristiche della vettura iscritta sono pienamente conformi alle prescrizioni del Regolamento Nazionale Vetture Sport. Il concorrente dovrà, inoltre, unire alla iscrizione due esemplari del Catalogo Ufficiale corrispondente al tipo e alla marca della vettura iscritta, dal quale si possano desumere tutti i dati necessari alla verifica e all'ammissione, nonchè una dichiarazione della Casa costruttrice, diretta alla F.A.S.I., che confermi l'esattezza dei dati del Catalogo e quanto richiesto all'art. 3, paragrafi a) b) c), del Regolamento Nazionale delle Vetture Sport.

**CARBURANTE**

Art. 6 - La scelta del carburante è libera.

Art. 7 - Le vetture ammesse verranno suddivise nelle seguenti classi di cilindrata:

Classe I fino a 750 cmc.
» II da 750 cmc. a 1100 cmc.
» III da 1100 cmc. a 1500 cmc.
» IV da 1500 cmc. a 2000 cmc.
» V da 2000 cmc. a 3000 cmc.

4

Alla chiusura delle iscrizioni verranno soppresse quelle classi in cui non vi fossero almeno tre vetture iscritte. In questo caso i concorrenti potranno partecipare nella classe superiore.

**CONCORRENTI e CONDUTTORI**

Art. 8 - Alla corsa potranno partecipare in qualità di concorrenti e conduttori tutti coloro che saranno muniti delle rispettive licenze internazionali 1940 - XVIII rilasciate dalla Federazione Automobilistica Sportiva Italiana o da Automobile Club estero affiliato all'A.I.A.C.R. Il concorrente che sia anche conduttore dovrà essere in possesso di entrambe le licenze internazionali.

**ISCRIZIONI**

Art. 9 - Le domande d'iscrizione, firmate dal concorrente, non saranno valide se non saranno inoltrate per iscritto o per telegramma, confermato con lettera raccomandata in pari data.

Le iscrizioni dovranno pervenire, in duplice copia, alla Federazione Automobilistica Sportiva Italiana, (ROMA Via Pó, 14) non oltre le ore 12 del giorno 15 aprile 1940 XVIII.

Le iscrizioni a tassa doppia resteranno aperte fino alle ore 12 del giorno 20 aprile 1940 - XVIII.

Tale termine è assolutamente improrogabile. Non sarà tenuto conto delle iscrizioni che perverranno dopo tale data o che non saranno accompagnate dalla tassa prescritta.

La tassa d'iscrizione è stabilita in L. 300 per ogni macchina. Ogni iscrizione dovrà essere redatta su apposito modulo fornito dal Reale Automobile Circolo d'Italia, Sede Provinciale di Brescia, sul quale dovranno risultare tutti i dati riferentesi alla macchina

unitamente all'indicazione del versamento della tassa d'iscrizione. È ammesso, però, che la designazione obbligatoria dei due conduttori venga fatta in data posteriore, purchè ciò non avvenga oltre le ore 12 del giorno 20 aprile.

**ASSICURAZIONI**

Art. 10 - Le domande d'iscrizione dovranno essere accompagnate dalla somma di L. 360 quale ammontare del premio dovuto per l'assicurazione della responsabilità Civile che verrà prestata con la Polizza aperta stipulata a speciali condizioni di favore dalla Sezione Nazionale Fascista Corridori con l'Anonima Infortuni di Milano, quale delegataria di un gruppo di Compagnie di Assicurazioni.

Le garanzie prestate dalla citata Polizza valgono per i seguenti massimali :

L. 225.000 per catastrofe
» 75.000 per persona
» 20.000 per danni a cose.

**DESIGNAZIONE DEI CONDUTTORI**

Art. 11 - Il concorrente ha il diritto di designare due conduttori per ciascuna vettura iscritta.

Su ogni vettura dovranno prendere posto due persone che saranno considerate alla stessa stregua in qualità di conduttori. Esse non potranno essere, per nessuna ragione sostituite, durante la corsa. Il ritiro lungo il percorso di uno dei due conduttori provocherà l'esclusione dalla classifica, e l'equipaggio sarà considerato solo agli effetti del tempo massimo.

In caso di indisponibilità di un conduttore per il giorno della corsa, un nuovo conduttore potrà essere ammesso dai Commissari Sportivi a condizione che egli sia

1° GRAN PREMIO BRESCIA DELLE MILLE MIGLIA 28 APRILE 1940-XVIII — Regolamento

proposto dal concorrente almeno due ore prima della partenza e che sia in possesso della licenza internazionale relativa.

La F.A.S.I. si riserva il diritto di rifiutare l'accettazione di un conduttore senza doverne far conoscere i motivi.

Art. 12 - Le Fabbriche o i Raggruppamenti Automobilistici che fossero in possesso di polizze di assicurazione aperte, contratte a copertura dei rischi di R.C. per i propri conduttori, potranno rimettere, entro il termine stabilito per la chiusura delle iscrizioni, le applicazioni relative in sostituzione dell'ammontare del premio di L. 360 dovuto.

In ogni caso le polizze dovranno esplicitamente stabilire che le Compagnie o Società d'assicurazione, in caso di sinistro, rinunciano ad ogni ricorso contro la F.A.S.I., contro il R.A.C.I. - Sede Centrale e Sedi Provinciali di Brescia - Cremona - Mantova - nonchè contro il Comitato Organizzatore, gli Ufficiali ed ogni altra persona preposta all'organizzazione della corsa.

La stipulazione della Polizza R.C. non solleva i concorrenti ed i conduttori dalle responsabilità civili in cui potrebbero eventualmente incorrere.

**SORTEGGIO**

Art. 13 - L'estrazione dei numeri da assegnarsi alle vetture, che avverrà per classe, in ordine progressivo di cilindrata, avrà luogo presso la Sede Provinciale del R.A.C.I. a Brescia, in Piazza della Vittoria, il giorno di martedì 23 Aprile 1940 - XVIII alle ore 10.

Il sorteggio verrà fatto col seguente ordine :
1° - Vetture di cilindrata da cmc. 750
2° » » » » 750 a 1100

3 - Vetture di cilindrata da cmc. 1100 a 1500
4 » » » » 1500 a 2000
5 » » » » 2000 a 3000

**NUMERI SULLE VETTURE**

Art. 14 - Ogni vettura dovrà portare, in modo chiaro e ben visibile, di grandezza proporzionata alla macchina, il numero di partenza secondo l'ordine determinato dall'estrazione a sorte (vedi art. n. 13):
a) sul radiatore ;
b) sul cofano d'ambo i lati;
c) posteriormente.

**VERIFICA DELLE VETTURE**

Art. 15 - Tutte le vetture dovranno essere sottoposte nei giorni di giovedì 25, venerdì 26 aprile, dalle ore 9 alle 19 e sabato 27 aprile, dalle ore 8 alle 17, presso il R.A.C.I., Sede Provinciale di Brescia, in Piazza della Vittoria, all'esame dei Commissari Sportivi e Tecnici per le opportune verifiche.

È in facoltà dei Commissari Tecnici di escludere quelle vetture che, a loro insindacabile giudizio, non presentassero sufficienti garanzie di efficienza e di sicurezza.

A garanzia di veridicità delle dichiarazioni fornite, dopo effettuata la corsa, i concorrenti dovranno lasciare le vetture a disposizione dei Commissari sino alla scadenza del termine utile per i reclami. In caso di inesatta dichiarazione il titolare perderà il diritto ai premi e sarà inoltre passibile di più gravi penalità secondo la valutazione della Federazione Automobilistica Sportiva Italiana. Comunque i Commissari Tecnici procederanno alla verifica delle vetture e della cilindrata delle stesse onde accertare che i premi previsti per ogni classe siano assegnati effettivamente secondo le cilindrate dichiarate.

Le vetture in attesa della verifica verranno ritirate in locale debitamente sorvegliato ed accessibile ai soli Commissari Sportivi e Tecnici.

Le vetture dovranno esser smontate a cura dei concorrenti stessi, la mattina del giorno 29 aprile. I concorrenti potranno assistere alle verifiche.

**Lo scappamento libero è ammesso, ma non dovrà essere volto verso terra.** Lo scappamento non dovrà sollevare polvere e sarà provato anche prima della partenza.

Ogni trasgressione alla lettera e allo spirito del «Regolamento Nazionale per Vetture Sport» comporterà l'esclusione dalla gara con riserva di più severe penalità come previsto dal Codice Sportivo Internazionale.

Art. 16 - Le prove del percorso potranno essere effettuate a scelta dei concorrenti, non essendo previste prove ufficiali. Durante le prove, che saranno fatte in circuito aperto al traffico, i conduttori dovranno attenersi scrupolosamente alle norme del codice della strada. Pertanto concorrenti e conduttori assumono tutte le responsabilità di ogni ordine derivanti dalla loro condotta durante le prove stesse.   **PROVE SUL PERCORSO**

Art. 17 - Le vetture partiranno una alla volta, dando la precedenza a quelle di cilindrata inferiore.   **PARTENZA**

Gli intervalli saranno stabiliti dopo la chiusura delle iscrizioni e fissati a giudizio del Direttore della Corsa secondo il numero delle macchine concorrenti.

Le partenze verranno date alla «Curva del Foro Boario» appena dopo il sottopassaggio della linea Milano Venezia circa 1 Km. prima del traguardo d'arrivo.

9

---

**RIFORNIMENTI E RIPARAZIONI**   Art. 18 - I rifornimenti e le riparazioni per i quali non sono fissati speciali condizioni nè limite di aiutanti, sono così distribuiti lungo il percorso:

Per le macchine di cilindrata 750 Guidizzolo
»        »        » 1100 Piadena
»        »        » 1500 Cremona
»        »        » oltre 1500 Brescia
» Squadre aventi macchine di diversa cilindrata   Bozzolo.

I rifornimenti dovranno svolgersi in appositi recinti costruiti a cura degli organizzatori nelle località sopraindicate. Ogni recinto rifornimento sarà posto sotto la sorveglianza dei Commissari di percorso. Ai posti di rifornimento potranno accedere solo le persone addette ai rifornimenti.

Eventuali operazioni di rifornimento o di riparazioni sono consentite anche lungo il percorso.

**OBBLIGHI DEI CONDUTTORI E DEI CONCORRENTI**   Art. 19 - Il conduttore ha l'obbligo di dare strada ogni qual volta gli venga richiesta dal conduttore che stia per sorpassarlo, o che, comunque, lo abbia raggiunto.

Il conduttore costretto a fermarsi sul percorso deve collocare la vettura sul ciglio destro della strada, in un punto dal quale sia visibile tempestivamente dai sopraggiungenti. Nelle curve dovrà collocare la vettura sul margine esterno. Il conduttore dovrà mantenere durante lo svolgimento della corsa un contegno corretto.

Il conduttore non può mettersi sulla traiettoria di un altro concorrente, che egli abbia sorpassato, se prima non abbia raggiunto su di esso un vantaggio di almeno 50 metri.

Le macchine ritirate non potranno uscire dal circuito che dopo la fine della corsa.

10

---

Art. 20 - Per il fatto stesso della sua iscrizione il concorrente si impegna per sè e per i suoi conduttori a conformarsi al presente Regolamento, alle circolari relative alle applicazioni di esse e alle decisioni dei Commissari Sportivi. Il Concorrente si impegna inoltre di riconoscere il Codice Sportivo Internazionale dell'A.I.A.C.R., suoi annessi, il Regolamento Nazionale Sportivo della Federazione Automobilistica Sportiva Italiana, ed il Regolamento per vetture "Sport Nazionali,,.

Il concorrente s'impegna altresì di riconoscere come sola giurisdizione competente la Federazione Automobilistica Italiana e si impegna di accettare le penalità alle quali egli potrebbe esporsi rivolgendosi ad altre giurisdizioni.

Art. 21 - La classifica della corsa sarà stabilita in base al minor tempo impiegato a compiere l'intero percorso ed i premi saranno attribuiti al concorrente titolare dell'iscrizione della vettura classificata.   **CLASSIFICA**

Art. 22 - Il tempo massimo per le varie classi è così stabilito:   **TEMPO MASSIMO**

Classe 1ª - Cilindrata fino a 750 cmc. media Km. 75
Classe 2ª - Cilindr. da 750 a 1100 cmc. media Km. 90
Classe 3ª - Cilindr. da 1100 a 1500 cmc. media Km. 95
Classe 4ª - Cilindr. da 1500 a 2000 cmc. media Km. 110
Classe 5ª - Cilindr. da 2000 a 3000 cmc. media Km. 120

Art. 23 - Saranno assegnati i seguenti premi in denaro:   **PREMI DI CLASSE**

Classe fino a 750 cmc.

    1° classificato L. 10.000
    2°     "     "    6.000

11

---

    3° classificato L. 5.000
    4°     "     "    3.000
    5°     "     "    2.500
    6°     "     "    2.000
    7°     "     "    1.000
    8°     "     "      800

    Totale L. 30.300

Classe da 750 a 1100 cmc.

    1° classificato L. 10.000
    2°     "     "    6.000
    3°     "     "    5.000
    4°     "     "    3.000
    5°     "     "    2.500
    6°     "     "    2.000
    7°     "     "    1.000
    8°     "     "      800

    Totale L. 30.300

Classe da 1100 a 1500 cmc.

    1° classificato L. 10.000
    2°     "     "    6.000
    3°     "     "    5.000
    4°     "     "    3.000
    5°     "     "    2.500
    6°     "     "    2.000
    7°     "     "    1.000
    8°     "     "      800

    Totale L. 30.300

12

Classe da 1500 a 2000 cmc.

| | | | |
|---|---|---|---|
| 1° classificato | L. | | 10.000 |
| 2° | " | " | 6.000 |
| 3° | " | " | 5.000 |
| 4° | " | " | 3.000 |
| 5° | " | " | 2.500 |
| 6° | " | " | 2.000 |
| 7° | " | " | 1.000 |
| 8° | " | " | 800 |
| | | Totale L. | 30.300 |

Classe da 2000 a 3000 cmc.

| | | | |
|---|---|---|---|
| 1° classificato | L. | | 10.000 |
| 2° | " | " | 6.000 |
| 3° | " | " | 5.000 |
| 4° | " | " | 3.000 |
| 5° | " | " | 2.500 |
| 6° | " | " | 2.000 |
| 7° | " | " | 1.200 |
| 8° | " | " | 800 |
| | | Totale L. | 30.500 |

## CLASSIFICA ASSOLUTA

| | | | |
|---|---|---|---|
| 1° classificato | L. | | 35.000 |
| 2° | » | » | 20.000 |
| 3° | » | » | 15.000 |
| | | Totale L. | 70.000 |

Tassa d'iscrizione Lire 300,— per ogni squadra, (oltre all'iscrizione individuale).
Alla squadra vincitrice verrà assegnata una artistica statua in bronzo.

Art. 26 - I premi verranno corrisposti ai vincitori dopo che la F. A. S. I. avrà omologato i risultati della corsa.

**RECLAMI E APPELLI**

Art. 27 - Il diritto di reclamare è riservato ai concorrenti. I reclami relativi alla classifica delle vetture o all'accettazione dei concorrenti e conduttori dovranno essere presentati prima della chiusura dei controlli di verifica; quelli relativi allo svolgimento della corsa, entro 5 ore dalla fine della corsa tenuto conto del tempo massimo stabilito dall'articolo 22 del Regolamento.
Ciascun reclamo dovrà essere fatto per iscritto e rimesso nelle mani di un Commissario Sportivo o del Direttore della corsa accompagnato dalla somma di L. 200 per ogni vettura od equipaggio contro i quali verrà presentato il reclamo stesso. Tale somma verrà restituita nel solo caso che il reclamo risulti fondato.

**RESPONSABILITÀ**

Art. 28 - Sia il concorrente che i due conduttori di ogni vettura, per il fatto stesso d'iscriversi e di partecipare alla corsa, riconoscono di esonerare e di ritenere sollevati la F.A.S.I. il R.A.C.I. Sede Centrale, le Sedi Provinciali di Brescia - Cremona - Mantova, nonchè gli organizzatori e le persone addette all'organizzazione da ogni responsabilità per qualsiasi incidente e danno che potesse avvenire prima e durante la manifestazione ad essi ed a terzi.

Fra tutti i classificati in tempo massimo che non avranno diritto ad alcuno dei premi precedenti, verrà divisa la somma di . . . . . L. 25.500
fino ad un massimo di L. 750,—

| | | |
|---|---|---|
| Totale dei premi in denaro . . . | L. | 247.200 |
| Contributo alla Cassa di Previdenza Corridori Automobilisti . . . | " | 7.800 |
| Totale Generale L. | | 255.000 |

Premi speciali verranno assegnati ai concorrenti di ogni classe che avranno compiuto il giro più veloce.
I premi sono cumulabili.

**PER I CLASSIFICATI in TEMPO MASSIMO** Art. 24 - Per ciascuna vettura classificata in base alle medie prescritte dall'articolo 22 verranno assegnate, oltre al premio in denaro, due medaglie in bronzo - conio speciale "Mille Miglia" - e due artistici diplomi.

**CLASSIFICA SQUADRE** Art. 25 - È istituita una speciale classifica riservata alle Fabbriche costruttrici e Gruppi Automobilistici, i quali possono concorrere con un numero illimitato di squadre. Ogni squadra sarà composta di tre macchine della stessa marca anche se di diversa cilindrata. I componenti di ciascuna squadra dovranno essere dichiarati all'atto delle verifiche.
La classifica verrà data dalla somma dei tempi ottenuti dalle tre vetture componenti la squadra. In caso che nessuna squadra arrivi al completo, la classifica verrà fatta in base alla somma dei migliori tempi ottenuti dalle due macchine arrivate.

I concorrenti si impegnano inoltre di non adire a vie legali per qualunque vertenza dovesse sorgere in dipendenza dello svolgimento della corsa e di riconoscere i Commissari Sportivi e la Federazione Automobilistica Sportiva Italiana come la sola giurisdizione sportiva competente, salvo il diritto di appello previsto nel Codice Sportivo Internazionale.

**DISPOSIZIONI GENERALI** Art. 29 - Per quanto non è contemplato nel presente Regolamento, vigono il Codice Sportivo Internazionale dell'A. I. A. C. R., i suoi Annessi e il Regolamento Nazionale Sportivo ed Annesso che i concorrenti dichiarano di conoscere e di accettare.
Gli organizzatori si riservano di far conoscere a mezzo di circolari speciali, tutte le prescrizioni che crederanno di dovere disporre relativamente alla applicazione del presente Regolamento.
Queste circolari, esplicative, avranno lo stesso effetto del presente Regolamento del quale faranno parte integrale.

IL PRESIDENTE DEL R. A. C. I·
Sede Provinciale di Brescia
FRANCO MAZZOTTI

Il Presidente della F. A. S. I
G. FURMANIK

44 *The poster and route of the Primo Gran Premio Brescia delle Mille Miglia, to be held on 28 April 1940.*

## 1° GRAN PREMIO BRESCIA
## DELLE MILLE MIGLIA

Exactly 50 years ago, on 28 April 1940, a race was run from Brescia which was destined to leave its mark on motoring history, a race which is remembered today for various reasons. Firstly for the fact that it saw the first car made entirely by Enzo Ferrari make its debut.

The race we are talking about was the First Brescia Grand Prix-Mille Miglia, which in reality was the 13th Mille Miglia.

This, the most famous road race in the world, was created at Brescia in 1927 and had been run with ever-increasing success until 1938 when, due to a serious accident at Bologna which left seven people dead, the government decided to suspend it indefinitely.

The measure had thrown the organisers of the race into panic, principally the founders: Renzo Castagneto, Giovanni Canestrini, Aymo Maggi, and Franco Mazzotti. These men were however soon busy finding a formula which could find a way round the govern-

*The letter from Enzo Ferrari sent to Renzo Castagneto, organiser of the race, to confirm the participation of the two Auto Avio Costruzioni cars, accompanied by two application forms with signatures of the two drivers.*

ment's ruling and could in some way decently resurrect their creation. One formula, it appears, was suggested to them by the driver and journalist, Giovanni Lurani. In April 1938 in the magazine 'Auto Italiana' he had proposed the transformation of the Mille Miglia from a road race (on the traditional course Brescia-Roma and back) to a race on a closed road circuit, of the type which was used at the beginning of this century for the Circuit of Brescia and the Coppa Florio.

That was how the original founders of the Mille Miglia came to ask the government for authorisation to organise a motor race at Brescia on a closed road circuit which would officially take the name of 'Primo Gran Premio Brescia delle Mille Miglia.'

Permission was granted and the indefatigable Renzo Castagneto, patron of all the previ-

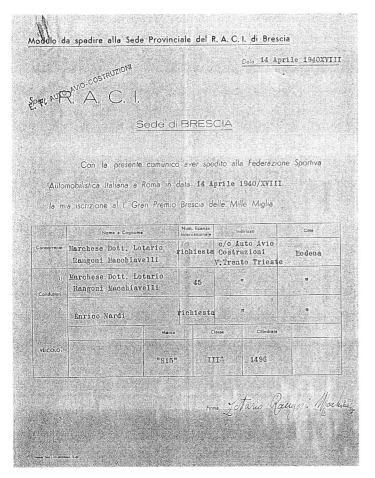

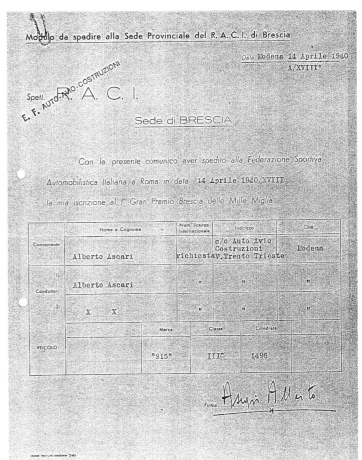

ous races in the series, immediately set himself to work organising the first 'Gran Premio' which was to be run on 28 April 1940.

The closed road circuit, to be lapped 9 times, was a large isosceles triangle, 165 kilometres long, with the apex at Brescia and the base angles at Cremona and Mantua.

The start, however, would not be from viale del Rebuffone in Brescia, the picturesque scene of the starts and finishes of the previous Mille Miglia races; it would be on the

# AUTO - AVIO COSTRUZIONI
## MODENA

## La nuova 815 - 8 cilindri 1500 cmc.

outskirts of the city. The road to Cremona began on the curve of the Foro Boario with the viale Duca degli Abruzzi. The finish line was also to be placed on this long street, together with the operating centre of the organisation. The course was entirely on the flat plain of Padano, where long straight roads with few curves cross the fertile countryside. It was therefore very fast, but included such hazards as four level-crossings, some very dangerous bends going through villages, and bumps and holes pretty well everywhere.

Renzo Castagneto lived up to his reputation as an organiser and, in the weeks prior to the race, the circuit was fitted out in the best possible way for the safety of both drivers and spectators. Castagneto, determined to carry the job out to perfection, surpassed himself, inventing and creating practically everything from a blank sheet of paper. This even included an authentic 'little city' on the finish line, which was intended to last just for the space of a morning.

**AUTO-AVIO COSTRUZIONI**

Enzo Ferrari

Modena-Italia

49

In particular, the patron had constructed a large stand from scaffolding. It was about 100 metres long, capable of housing 3,000 people and which had in the middle an impressive 7-storey tower, 25 metres high and decorated with the characteristic red arrows reserved for the organisation. The tower would house the race controllers, the timers, the telephone switchboard, foreign and Italian journalists, the radio station (E.I.A.R.) and the commentator, who would give out the news over loudspeakers. In front of the principal stand a gigantic hoarding, 9 metres high and 50 metres long, was erected giving the timings by which the spectators would easily be able to follow the course of the race.

Then other smaller stands were built, together with a very useful aerial footway and even a large amusement park with

*An advertisement for the 815 as it appeared in the programme for the 1940 Gran Premio Brescia delle Mille Miglia, produced by the organisers on the occasion of the great event. As well as information and specification tables, the programme included many articles by important writers, journalists and technicians from the motoring world.*

bars, restaurants, car-parks and an area set aside for bookmakers where it was possible

to bet on the outcome of the race. Finally, pit garages for the competitors were built be-

hind which a large paddock was set aside for the cars to gather at the end of the event.

The race was fixed for Sunday 28 April and during the preceding days, following tradi-

tion, the cars entered were scrutineered in the piazza della Vittoria. In the Spring of 1940

things in Europe had unfortunately come to a head. Germany, having attacked Poland,

found itself at war with France and Britain. Italy was on the brink of an abyss into which

it was soon to be plunged. That day, however - and this was really rather strange - cars,

drivers, mechanics and journalists were present from some of

the countries at war, and everything was conducted as normal,

in the name of a common sporting ideal strong enough to

overcome even the most bitter political conflicts. The race was

*Brescia, 28 April 1940,*
*6.20 a.m.*
*The secretary of the*
*National Fascist Party, Ettore*
*Muti, surrounded by*
*high-ranking officers of the*
*Militia, gives the*
*starting signal to the*
*Rangoni-Nardi car...*

51

open only to cars in the 'Sport Nazionale' category (those Italian

*... and a minute later, the Ascari-Minozzi 815 takes to the road.*

and foreign cars which qualified), and for this reason only cars

without superchargers were entitled to be entered and presented in Piazza della Vittoria.

Italy was banking on the success of the strong Alfa Romeo team, already victorious in

ten previous Mille Miglias, which lined up four 2500s with bodywork by Touring of Mi-

lan: three Spyders (driven by the teams of Biondetti-Stefani, Farina-Mambelli, Pintacuda-

Sanesi) and a Berlina, driven by Trossi-Lucchi. These were cars which could reach 185

km/h in the Spyder version and 196 km/h in the Berlina.

France was represented by two, powerful works Delage 3000s, driven by the Italian

teams Taruffi-Chinetti and Comotti-Rosa, and capable of reaching 200 km/h, despite body-

work of typically transalpine conception which was far from aerodynamic.

Finally, Germany had marshalled a squadron of five 2-litre BMW's (the famous 328), machines to be feared but inferior on paper to the more powerful Alfas and Delages. Three of the BMWs were Spyders (Wencher-Scholtz, Briem-Richter, Brudes-Roese). Two on the other hand were Berlinas: the first with Touring body, and back from a brilliant victory in the Le Mans 24-hour race of 1939, was driven by von Hanstein and Baumer. The second, with a body made by the same firm in accordance with the most advanced aerodynamic criteria, was driven by the Italian team of Lurani-Cortese. The real speed of these cars had not been revealed, and when during the race this became apparent, it was an unpleasant surprise for their competitors.

If the most interesting cars appeared to be the Alfas and Delages (also considered by some to be the outright favourites), and of course the German BMWs, there was yet another

Italian car, which attracted everyone's attention at the time. It was the 815, which had been built in only four months by Enzo Ferrari at his own factory, Auto Avio Costruzioni.

There were two examples entered, both open cars with a Touring body, entrusted to Ascari-Minozzi and Rangoni-Nardi. At the time, it was described by the magazine 'Auto Italiana' in the following manner: "In the 1500 cc class... the competition will immediately take on a most unusual interest with the debut of the first cars constructed at Modena by Enzo Ferrari ... baptised with the name 815 ... The two Ferrari cars are at the moment complete strangers to the effects of the race, and above all to the staying power required by the severe distance, but on paper they have the opportunity

*The 815 of Rangoni-Nardi photographed on a spectacular curve during the Brescia Gran Premio Mille Miglia. The car withdrew on the penultimate lap because of rear axle failure.*

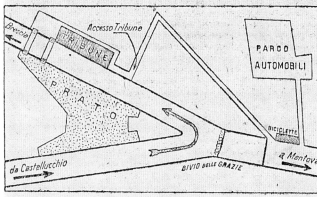

# AUTOMOBILISMO
## L'organizzazione del G. P. Brescia

La curva a forcina al vertice presso Mantova

# I servizi radio

Un completo servizio radiofonico funzionerà durante lo svolgimento del 1. G. P. Brescia delle Mille Miglia. Le fasi della corsa saranno radiotrasmesse dall'E.I.A.R., e cronisti saranno i colleghi Raffaello Guzman e Vittorio Veltroni. Il giornale-radio farà inoltre un ampio servizio fornendo continuamente notizie negli sviluppi della corsa.

of a victory of the first order". Even so the participation of the 815's remained in doubt right up until the eve of scrutineering, when Ferrari telephoned Castagneto and confirmed that he would be present at Brescia as he had promised, but he also said, "for a good try-out", because he knew that it would be difficult for the two cars to finish the race.

So, in summary: in the 3000 cc class the Alfas would do battle with the Delages; in the 2000 cc class the BMWs would have no rivals; in the 1500 cc class the fight would be between the 815 and the Fiats and Lancia Aprilias; and in the 1100 and 750 classes there would not be a battle between different manufacturers, since all the cars entered were Fiats, but between private entrants with some extraordinary variations in engine modifications and bodywork.

It must be said that this wartime Mille Miglia was historic also for the rich and varied range of the bodywork of the cars that took part in it - a sign of the dedicated, fruitful research and experiment which then, unfortunately, had to be interrupted during the

years of war. Finally, the night of 27 April arrived: the moment of departure. The crowd waited impatiently for the first cars, those of the 750 cc class, and, at one minute past four precisely, the first Fiat Topolino, a red barchetta with the number 2, noisily took to the road.

Then, the 1100 cc cars left; the 815's and the 1500 cc Lancia Aprilias, the BMW 328

squadron, and finally at dawn, the Alfas and the Delages.

The cars left the curve of the Foro Boario on the edge of Brescia and headed for Cremona along an endless series of fast tree-lined straights, interrupted by the occasional easy bend. In the

*The 815 number 65 of Rangoni-Nardi photographed on a spectacular curve during the Brescia Gran Premio Mille Miglia. The car withdrew on the penultimate lap because of rear axle failure.*

open countryside there was little to fear, while danger lurked in the villages, where tight and treacherous bends suddenly appeared.

Then, before Cremona, there was the long ring-road which the local leader, Farinacci had had built expressly for the race: a great parabolic curve at its entrance; a wide straight of two kilometres, as smooth as a billiard ball, where the cars touched top speed (and where Ferrari had positioned his headquarters); and another great parabolic curve at the exit.

Once past Cremona the cars headed for Mantua running through more long straights in the farming country of the Padana plain. On improvised stands, at the windows of houses, perched in trees and on publicity hoardings, people gathered at the sides of the road, impervious to danger in their enthusiasm.

The stretch from Cremona to Mantua was also not without its perils, however. The cars had to go over three level-crossings,

# Gazzetta dello Sport

**SECONDA EDIZIONE**

**SABATO E DOMENICA 27-28 Aprile**

— Anno XVIII —

*Un numero Cent. 30*

Esce tutti i giorni esclusa la domenica
Spedizione in abbonamento postale
★ ★ ★

| Prezzi e combinazioni d'abbonamento | GAZZETTA DELLO SPORT | | | GAZZETTA DELLA DOMENICA | | | GAZZETTA SPORT e GAZZETTA della DOMENICA | | |
|---|---|---|---|---|---|---|---|---|---|
| | Anno | Semestre | Trimestre | Anno | Semestre | Trimestre | Anno | Semestre | Trimestre |
| ITALIA — Impero e Colonie L. | 75.— | 38.— | 20.— | 12.— | 7.— | 4.— | 86.— | 44.— | 23.— |
| ESTERO ....... » | 160.— | 81.— | 41.— | 24.— | 13.— | 7.— | 180.— | 92.— | 46.— |

NUMERI ARRETRATI
« Gazzetta dello Sport »: cent. 60
CARTOLINE SPORTIVE
10 cartoline lusso assortite .... L. 1,20
10 cartoline campioni del ciclismo » 1,—

## SERENITA' FORZA E ARDIMENTO DELLO SPORT FASCISTA

# ...iglia è rinata nel fausto segno
# ...AN PREMIO BRESCIA

— Circuito Brescia-Cremona-Mantova km. 165 da ripetersi nove volte (km. 1485) - Partenze dalle ore 4,01 alle 7,26

...ci dell'automobilismo
...va generazione
...o le imprese dei pionieri

**I PILOTI DELLA B.M.W.**

## AUTOMOBILISMO
## IL G. P. di Brescia
### Numeri di corsa ed ore di partenza

BRESCIA, 26. — Ecco i numeri di corsa e l'ordine di partenza dei concorrenti al I Gran Premio Brescia delle Mille Miglia.

**CLASSE I: fino a 750 cmc.**

| | ORE |
|---|---|
| 1. Carnevali-Faccanoni (Fiat) | 4.01 |
| 2. « Forse » - « Chissà » (Fiat) | 4.02 |
| 3. Civit-Ghersi F. (Fiat) | 4.03 |
| 4. Bortolon-Monaco (Fiat) | 4.04 |
| 5. Grassi-X (Fiat) | 4.05 |
| 6. Francesconi-Maceri (Fiat) | 4.06 |
| 7. Cortesi-Parravicini (Fiat) | 4.07 |
| 8. Bossini-Foschetti (Fiat) | 4.08 |
| 9. Ferniani-Lama (Fiat) | 4.09 |
| 10. Pasquini Oscar - Pasquini Walter (Fiat) | 4.10 |
| 11. Franco - « Civetta » (Fiat) | 4.11 |
| 12. « Trentanove » - Manni (Fiat) | 4.12 |
| 13. X. X. (Fiat) | 4.13 |
| 14. Brinchetti-Spotti L. (Fiat) | 4.14 |
| 15. Broglia-Crivelli (Fiat) | 4.15 |
| 16. « Gracco » - Polidori (Fiat) | 4.16 |
| 17. X. X. (Fiat) | 4.17 |
| 18. Venturelli-Ceroni (Fiat) | 4.18 |
| 19. Capra-Selva (Fiat) | 4.19 |
| 20. Fumagalli-Castiglioni (Fiat) | 4.20 |
| 21. Donati R.-Garzi (Fiat) | 4.21 |
| 22. Quadri-Sertorio (Fiat) | 4.22 |
| 23. Piau-Carraroli (Fiat) | 4.23 |
| 24. « Porto Flip »-Massa (Fiat) | 4.24 |
| 25. Meomartini-Gatti (Fiat) | 4.25 |
| 26. Herkuleys-X. (M. G.) | 4.26 |

**CLASSE II: fino a 1100 cmc.**

| | ORE |
|---|---|
| 27. Goriup-Schoss (Fiat) | 5.10 |
| 28. Benozzo-Arancio (Fiat) | 5.11 |
| 29. Licini-Tettamenti (Fiat) | 5.12 |
| 30. Crotti-Montorsi (Fiat) | 5.13 |
| 31. Franchetti-Cappellotto (Fiat) | 5.14 |
| 32. Pierini-Bossi (Fiat) | 5.15 |
| 33. Gilera-X. (Fiat) | 5.16 |
| 34. Comirato Alberto e Lia (Fiat) | 5.17 |
| 35. Rossi-Giuliani (Fiat) | 5.18 |
| 36. Bertagna-Lasigni (Fiat) | 5.19 |
| 37. Adanti-Baccarini (Fiat) | 5.20 |
| 38. « Setto » - « Nani » (Fiat) | 5.21 |
| 39. Beltracchini-Corradi (Fiat) | 5.22 |
| 40. Zordan-Crivellari (Fiat) | 5.23 |
| 41. Palmieri-Bronzoni (Fiat) | 5.24 |
| 42. Ruggeri-Danzi (Fiat) | 5.25 |
| 43. Marangoni-Moscatelli (Fiat) | 5.26 |
| 44. Priario-Tanea (Fiat) | 5.27 |
| 45. Tellini-Ghelfi (Fiat) | 5.28 |
| 46. Ferruzzi-Cavanni (Fiat) | 5.29 |
| 47. Fonticelli-Zanella (Fiat) | 5.30 |
| 48. Lanzini-Bassi (Fiat) | 5.31 |
| 49. Donati A.-Massimiani (Fiat) | 5.32 |

| | ORE |
|---|---|
| 50. Catanese-X (Fiat) | 5.33 |
| 51. Clocchiatti Luciano e Aldo (Fiat) | 5.34 |
| 52. Della Cella-Avanzo M. Antonietta (Fiat) | 5.35 |
| 53. Zanussi-X (Fiat) | 5.36 |
| 54. Arselli-Bandini (Fiat) | 5.37 |

**CLASSE III: fino a 1500 cmc.**

| | ORE |
|---|---|
| 55. Placido-Celasco (Lancia) | 6.10 |
| 56. D'Ambrosio-Guerrini (Lancia) | 6.11 |
| 57. Proto-Fiore (Lancia) | 6.12 |
| 58. « Val » - « Piuco » (Lancia) | 6.13 |
| 59. De Martino-Redisma (Lancia) | 6.14 |
| 60. Marelli-Varallo (Lancia) | 6.15 |
| 61. Bosco-Balma (Lancia) | 6.16 |
| 62. « Viorbi » - Villa Paolo (id.) | 6.17 |
| 63. Bassi-Furlelli (Lancia) | 6.18 |
| 64. Ruggero-Wurzburger (Fiat) | 6.19 |
| 65. Rangoni-Nardi (815) | 6.20 |
| 66. Ascari-Minozzi (815) | 6.21 |
| 67. Leoncini-Guidotti (Lancia) | 6.22 |
| 68. « Ariano » - Forti (Lancia) | 6.23 |
| 69. Bracco-Casalegno (Lancia) | 6.24 |

**CLASSE IV: fino a 2000 cmc.**

| | ORE |
|---|---|
| 70. Haustein-Baumer (B.M.W.) | 6.40 |
| 71. Wencher-Scholtz (B.M.W.) | 6.42 |
| 72. Brien-Richter (B.M.W.) | 6.44 |
| 73. Lurani-Cortese (B.M.W.) | 6.46 |
| 74. Brudes-Roese (B.M.W.) | 6.48 |

**CLASSE V: fino a 3000 cmc.**

| | ORE |
|---|---|
| 75. Villoresi G. - X (Lancia-Astura) | 7.00 |
| 76. Trossi-Lurchi (Alfa Romeo) | 7.02 |
| 77. Taruffi-Chinetti (Delage) | 7.04 |
| 78. Boratto-X (Alfa Romeo) | 7.06 |
| 79. Biondetti-Stefani (Alfa Romeo) | 7.08 |
| 80. Chiodi-De Giorgi (Alfa Romeo) | 7.10 |
| 81. Dusio-Boninsegni (Alfa Romeo) | 7.12 |
| 82. Pintacuda-Sanesi (Alfa Romeo) | 7.14 |
| 83. Canestrini - Cattaneo (Alfa Romeo) | 7.16 |
| 84. Farina-Mandelli (Alfa Romeo) | 7.18 |
| 85. Cornaggia-Cavazzoni (Alfa Romeo) | 7.20 |
| 86. Comotti-Rosa (Delage) | 7.22 |
| 87. Tassara-Sacchetti (Alfa Romeo) | 7.24 |
| 88. Romano Emilio-X (Alfa Romeo) | 7.26 |

28 Aprile 1940-XVIII • **I EDIZIONE** ★

# ...ella Domenica

ABBONAMENTI

| | ITALIA-IMPERO-COLONIE: | ANNO SEM. | ESTERO: | ANNO SEM. |
|---|---|---|---|---|
| | La Gazzetta della Domenica L. | 12 L. 7 | | L. 24 L. 13 |
| | La Gazzetta della Domenica — L. | 84 L. 44 | | |
| | e Gazzetta della Domenica — L. | | | L. 180 L. 92 |

NUMERI ARRETRATI: Cent. 60

...): L. 5 per mm. d'altezza, larghezza una colonna; per posizioni ...larghezza da 1 a 8 colonne) esclusa la prima pagina, prezzi ... ecc. L. 10 per mm.: ECONOMICI: vedi rubriche; ...ARANCIO, ecc. L. 10 per mm.: ...amministrazione si riserva il diritto di rifiutare quegli ordini che ... vanno diretti esclusivamente all'UNIONE PUBBLICITA' ...elefoni dal 12-451 al 12-455 e succursali...

...OBILISMO
...ate
...nale
...i Brescia

...dalle 4.01 alle 7.26)
...ore di partenza

52. Della Cella-Avanzo M. Antonietta (Fiat)    5.35
53. Zanussi-X (Fiat)    5.36
54. Arselli-Bandini (Fiat)    5.37

57

PRIMA EDIZIONE

MERCOLEDÌ
24
Aprile
— Anno XVIII —
Un numero Cent. 30

Ecco tutti i giorni escluso la domenica
Spedizione in abbonamento postale

## AUTOMOBILISMO

## Le posizioni giro per giro

| | 1° GIRO km. 165 | 2° GIRO km. 230 | 3° GIRO km. 495 | 4° GIRO km. 660 | 5° GIRO km. 825 | 6° GIRO km. 990 | 7° GIRO km. 1155 | 8° GIRO km. 1320 | 9° GIRO km. 1485 |
|---|---|---|---|---|---|---|---|---|---|
| **CLASSE 750** | Venturelli (112.213) Ferniani Cortesi Brinchetti Franco | Venturelli (109.640) Cortesi Ferniani Brinchetti Quadri | Cortesi (112.099) Venturelli Brinchetti Franco Quadri | Venturelli (113.080) Cortesi Brinchetti Franco Quadri | Venturelli (112.972) Cortesi Brinchetti Quadri Franco | Venturelli (113.040) Cortesi Brinchetti Quadri Franco | Cortesi (113.603) Venturelli Quadri Franco Brinchetti | Venturelli (114.063) Cortesi Quadri Franco Forse | |
| **CLASSE 1100** | Sette (130.657) Bertani Ruggeri Goriup Fioruzzi | Bertani (130.945) Ruggeri Sette Fioruzzi Goriup | Fioruzzi (131.136) Bertani Goriup Lanzini Donati | Fioruzzi (133.019) Bertani Goriup Lanzini Zordan | Fioruzzi (133.187) Bertani Marangoni Lanzini Zordan | Fioruzzi (132.021) Bertani Marangoni Lanzini Zordan | Fioruzzi (132.572) Bertani Marangoni Lanzini Zordan | Fioruzzi (131.993) Bertani Marangoni Zordan Lanzini | Fioruzzi (132.720) Bertani Marangoni Zordan Lanzini |
| **CLASSE 1500** | Ascari (143.771) Rangoni Bracco Minetti Bosco | Rangoni (141.692) Leoncini Minetti D'Ambrosio Viorbi | Rangoni (143.125) Leoncini Minetti Viorbi D'Ambrosio | Rangoni (142.720) Leoncini Viorbi Minetti Ruggero | Rangoni (142.738) Leoncini D'Ambrosio Minetti Ruggero | Rangoni (142.716) Leoncini D'Ambrosio Ruggero Bassi | Rangoni (141.654) Leoncini D'Ambrosio Ruggero Bassi | D'Ambrosio (126.292) Ruggero Bassi Proto | |
| **CLASSE 2000** | Haustein (163.359) Lurani Brudes Brien Wencher | Haustein (167.940) Lurani Brudes Brien Wencher | Haustein (167.624) Brudes Brien Lurani Wencher | Haustein (169.176) Brudes Brien Wencher Lurani | Haustein (169.393) Brudes Brien Wencher Lurani | Haustein (168.682) Brudes Brien Wencher Lurani | Haustein (167.913) Brudes Wencher Brien Lurani | Haustein (167.636) Brudes Wencher Brien | Haustein (166.723) Brudes Brieñ Wencher |
| **CLASSE 3000** | Comotti (159.812) Farina Biondetti Trossi Tassara | Farina (161.547) Comotti Biondetti Trossi Pintacuda | Farina (162.274) Comotti Biondetti Trossi Pintacuda | Farina (161.937) Biondetti Comotti Trossi Pintacuda | Farina (162.469) Trossi Biondetti Comotti Pintacuda | Farina (162.785) Trossi Pintacuda Biondetti Chiodi | Farina (162.502) Biondetti Pintacuda Trossi Chiodi | Farina (162.408) Biondetti Pintacuda Trossi Chiodi | Farina (162.028) Biondetti Pintacuda Trossi Chiodi |

I numeri tra parentesi, indicano le medie chilometriche

encounter bumps and holes which caused some dangerous acrobatics, and negotiate treacherous bends in crowded villages until, at the Le Grazie section a little before Mantua, the course of the circuit veered suddenly to the left, northwards, and went as far as Goito along a rutted and primitive road.

CONI

From there, the cars headed directly for Brescia, racing along more fast straights across the plain. They got through the last few dangerous bends, including Foro Boario, at the edge of Brescia, and crossed the start/finish line to begin the struggle against time all over again.

At the end of the first lap, von Hanstein's BMW Berlina flashed across the line in 1 hour, 58 seconds, at an average speed, better than anyone predicted, of 163.359 km/h. He headed Comotti's Delage (the only one left, because Taruffi had to retire due to melted bearings) and Farina's Alfa. Lurani (BMW) was fourth, Biondetti (Alfa) fifth, while the other Spyder BMWs occupied seventh, eighth and ninth positions in a tight group. Von Hanstein's exploit impressed greatly, but few people

59

would have put their money on the young German driver to win, since the race was still very long and everyone was waiting for a strong come-back by the Alfas. Instead, the total superiority of the BMW team that day dashed Italian hopes.

*On the opposite page, Fascist party official Roberto Farinacci exchanges a couple of words with Alberto Ascari. In the centre, Enzo Ferrari and the Marchese Lotario Rangoni Machiavelli, first driver of the 815. Above, Ettore Muti gives the starting signal. At his side the official timekeeper Bonfanti from Cremona.*

The two Ferrari 815s were quite astonishing, being placed 12th and 13th, just behind the favourites at the head of their class and in front of some bigger-engined and more fancied cars.

At the end of the second lap, von Hanstein's BMW was still in the lead. Moreover, the German driver had gone round in less than an hour, and raised the average speed to 172.815 km/h, this time casting serious doubts as to the final outcome of the race.

Another BMW had moved up into second place - Lurani's Berlina - while Farina, with the first of the Alfas, had stayed in third place ahead of Comotti's Delage. Rangoni's 815, for its part, had gained two positions and continued to run very strongly, hitting over than 175 km/h in places while Ascari's car unfortunately had to retire owing to the broken rocker-arm.

During the third lap, von Hanstein's Berlina did even better, and zoomed under the finish banner at an astonishing average of 174.102 km/h, quashing any of its rivals' ambitions. Farina's Alfa had come up into second place, Biondetti was third, but the cars with the four-leaf clover continued to lose ground, and right on their tails they had the tight, menacing group of the other BMWs.

But Rangoni with the 815 stuck tenaciously to his 11th place, by now increasing outdistancing the other cars in his class.

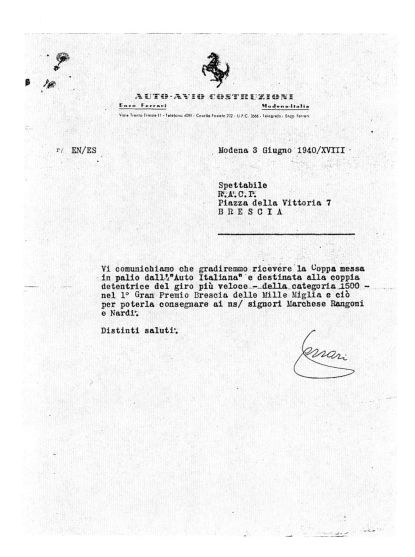

And from then on the race at its height saw little change ... Von Hanstein's BMW with superb bodywork by Touring continued unchallenged in the lead until the end, slowing down only a little for the sake of prudence; while behind him the bitter struggle went on between Comotti's Delage, the Alfas and the other BMWs.

Unfortunately Rangoni in the 815 had to drop out in the eighth lap, because of damage to the rear axle arising from the hurried preparation. He had moved up into tenth place and was continuing to dominate the rest of his class.

Then Lurani retired in open country, and together with him many other competitors with engines that had broken under the fierce pace which the leaders were forcing.

So, at 3.35 in the afternoon, while ominous black clouds were bearing down on the circuit, the BMW of Fritz Huschke von Hanstein victoriously crossed the finishing line in 8 hours 54 minutes and 46 seconds, an extraordinary average of 166.723 km/h, ahead of Farina's Alfa which was a quarter of an hour behind, and the BMW Spyder of Brudes.

Biondetti's Alfa was classified fourth; the BMWs of Briem and Wencher fifth and sixth. It was even put about that the

*The authoritative journal 'L'auto italiana' put up a trophy for the fastest lap in the 1500 class. Curiously, it was not awarded during the prize-giving and Enzo Ferrari had to write a couple of polite letters to the organisers insisting on it being sent to him.*

BMWs would have been able to do even better if they had not been deliberately slowed down by their directors so as not to humiliate the Italians. Although they had not yet entered the war, they had nevertheless clearly expressed support for Germany in the preceding months.

Today, half a century later, that race has an important place in the history of motoring. The first 'Gran Premio Brescia delle Mille Miglia' in 1940, boasts the unbeaten record of having been the fastest race in the world on a closed road circuit: perhaps more significantly it was the race that saw the advent of the first Ferrari in history.

In conclusion, that day a seed had been sown with the 815 which would bear many fruits. A man's dream was beginning to become a reality - a reality which as we all know, is well and truly alive today. A great sporting legend of our times had been born.

However, on that splendid Sunday 50 years ago, there was certainly no-one who could guess what would happen in the future. After the race had ended, came the joyous moment of the prize-giving, and then, as the weather was now worsening, the 'little city' built by Renzo Castagneto to last but 'the space of a morning' slowly and rather sadly emptied. So, at the first shadows of evening, the curtain closed on the last motor race of 1940, and everyone went away, each to his own destiny.

A destiny, sadly, of darkness.

*The BMW of the winners Hanstein-Baumer crossing the finishing line. In the background is the enormous hoarding giving the positions, 50 metres long and 9 metres high, which had been built to enable spectators to follow the race.*

*The Alfa Romeo 2500 number 84 of Farina-Mambelli which came second overall. Scrutineering took place in the piazza della Vittoria at Brescia. After the finish, the winners Hanstein and Baumer.*

64        *This photograph is the only one which shows the two 815s of Rangoni and Ascari together. It was taken by Corrado Millanta.*

# THE DRIVERS

# LOTARIO RANGONI MACCHIAVELLI

The Marchese Lotario Alfonso Rangoni Machiavelli belonged to an ancient and illustrious Modenese family. Born on 27 July 1913 in Florence, he spent his childhood and adolescence in the family house at Spilamberto, a few kilometres from Modena. Having finished his studies (gaining two degrees, one in law and the other in social and political sciences,) he began to work on the family's estates.

Always a great sportsman, he began to race cars in 1936 with a Fiat Balilla, obtaining good results and even winning an Italian Championship.

He then went on to Alfa Romeo, with whom he took part brilliantly in important competitions such as the Targa Abruzzo race with a 2500, together with the Modenese Nando Righetti.

*There were slight differences of appearance in Lotario Rangoni Machiavelli's car, particularly with regard to the radiator-grill. The aristocrat from Modena poses by his 815, smiling proudly.*

Later, unsatisfied with his Alfa, which he thought too heavy, he turned to Enzo Ferrari, at that time still working for the Milanese company, to see if he could provide him with a lighter and more competitive machine. The Alfa Romeo 2500 prepared by Ferrari served Machiavelli well. Thus a fruitful friendship was born that was destined to last a long time.

In 1939 the young Lotario asked Enzo Ferrari to build him a car to take part in the Mille Miglia and Ferrari provided him with the 815, the first 'creation' of Auto Avio Costruzioni, the company founded in Modena to get round the bans imposed on Ferrari by Alfa Romeo.

In the 1940 Gran Premio Brescia delle Mille Miglia, in which he participated with Enrico Nardi in the 815, he had to retire because of mechanical problems. It was the last race Rangoni Machiavelli could compete in before leaving for the war. Fond of aeroplanes and possessing a pilot's licence, he was made a flight lieutenant at Pistoia. And it was there that on 2 October 1942, while testing a new aircraft, he crashed and lost his life.

# ENRICO NARDI

**E**nrico Nardi was born in Bologna on the 31 January 1907. He was educated at Turin, where he moved with his family whilst still a small child, and where he had his first experience behind a steering wheel. In 1935, having returned to Emilia, he began work as a test-driver with the Scuderia Ferrari which at that time was racing Alfas.

With the closure of the Scuderia, Ferrari still continued to work for Alfa Romeo, becoming director of 'Alfa Corse'. Ferrari's and Alfa's objective at that time was to compete with the German teams which for some years had dominated the international scene. Ferrari gathered round him a group of excellent technicians: Gioachino Colombo, Luigi Bazzi, Alberto Massimino and Federico Giberti with whom he produced a legendary car, the Alfa Romeo 158.

Enrico Nardi was always present as a test-driver and at times, because of his previous experience, also as adviser; his contributions were a determining factor when setting up. It was no coincidence that he was the first to take it out onto the track, on 5 May 1938 at Monza. The debut of the 158 soon became a triumph.

Relations between Ferrari and Alfa Romeo came stormily to an end in 1938 and, in order to get round the ban on building cars and racing them imposed on him by Portello, Ferrari founded the firm of Auto Avio Costruzioni in Modena.

The 815 was produced there by Alberto Massimino, Vittorio Bellentani and with the

68

active participation of Nardi, both as adviser and test driver. Ferrari himself wanted Nardi to do the testing, and on the roads of Emilia he undertook tens of thousands of kilometres to refine the car in preparation for the first Brescia Grand Prix.

Enrico Nardi was present at this historic competition, at the side of Marchese Lotario Rangoni Machiavelli. Unfortunately, after a race driven brilliantly, the Rangoni-Nardi team was forced to retire because of mechanical failure. The result was still good though, because the car's potential had been fully brought to light.

Differing interests and some quarrels ended the collaboration of Ferrari and Nardi in 1946. But they were to make up later in 1957, when Nardi, who had become the most prized maker of steering wheels in the world, was chosen to be the official supplier to the Maranello company. This renewed a friendship that was to last without interruption until Nardi's death in 1966.

# ALBERTO ASCARI

**A**lberto Ascari, son of the famous driver Antonio, was born in Milan on 13 July 1918. In 1936, when he was just 18, he began to give vent to his passion for speed by racing motorbikes. He appeared in 27 events, riding variously on Sertum, Gilera and Bianchi motorcycles, and winning a good dozen times.

His real aspirations, however, were to go on to four wheels and follow in his father's footsteps; and so he turned to Enzo Ferrari to commission from him a car with which to

take part in the 1940 Mille Miglia. Ferrari, who appreciated the gifts of Alberto's father, Antonio, with whom he had been a rival in competition but a friend in life, had no difficulty pleasing the son. The 815, produced in a very short time, was launched at the start of the race on 28 April 1940. For Alberto, who had acquired the machine, it was his debut in the motoring world.

The young driver (not yet 22) had inherited the impetuousness of his father and started very fast, putting himself solidly in the lead of his class. Unfortunately the event ended unluckily for him when a broken rocker-arm forced him to retire, but the trial had already shown his talents. After the war Ascari took up racing again in 1947, at first with Cisitalia and Maserati (with the single exception of the French Grand Prix at Reims where he raced an Alfa 158).

In 1949, on 12 June to be precise, he made his debut in a Ferrari at Bari. With this car Ascari scored his greatest victories and for two consecutive years he won two World Drivers' Championships (1952 and 1953). In 1954 he moved to Lancia and carried off a prestigious victory in that year's Mille Miglia with a Lancia Sport, though he didn't have the same luck with the Turin company's Formula 1 cars.

70

During the 1955 Monte Carlo Grand Prix he ended up in the sea with a broken nose.

Four days later, on 26 May at Monza, he asked to do a few laps in Eugenio Castellotti's 3-litre Ferrari; he was practising on the circuit.

After a couple of laps, through reasons which are still unknown today, he crashed and was killed.

**GIOVANNI MINOZZI**

**G**iovanni Minozzi is the least known of the four who took part in the 1940 Mille Miglia in the two 815s produced by Auto Avio Costruzioni. Born at Castel d'Ario in the province of Mantua on 29 January 1898, he belonged to a family which produced two great champions: Antonio and Alberto Ascari. Giovanni's father, Amilcare Minozzi, had in fact married one of Antonio Ascari's sisters, Marianna, with whom he had two children.

The passion for motors and racing showed itself early in the young Minozzi who, inspired by the example of his celebrated and daring uncle Antonio, began to frequent the racing-car scene.

During the twenties and thirties, without scoring any major successes he won quiet fame as a driver, racing mostly Alfas. His numerous competitions and the friendship he enjoyed with many of the greatest drivers of the time enriched his experience and made him the man most suited to sit beside his cousin Alberto Ascari, who had decided to fol-

low in his father's footsteps and go from two to four wheels. The young Alberto, impetuous and fiery like his father, had already scored many brilliant victories in motorcycle racing but was still relatively inexperienced in the field of car racing. So it was proposed to the 42-year-old Minozzi that he sit at Alberto's side in the Primo Gran Premio delle Mille Miglia in order to temper the youthful impetuosity of his cousin's character with his experience and circumspection. Although they did not finish the race the first appearance of Alberto in a racing car showed what his real potential was.

Giovanni Minozzi retired from competition a few years later, but that race in 1940, remained indelibly printed in his memory even though it lasted only a few kilometres.

*Marianna, Antonio Ascari's sister and mother of Giovanni Minozzi, Alberto's cousin.*
*Opposite, Giovanni Minozzi at the wheel of an Alfa Romeo, in which he achieved good results in several races.*

74    *Advertising brochure for the machine tools produced by Ferrari's Auto Avio Costruzioni.*

Scuderia **Ferrari**
auto-avio costruzioni
Modena

I-3/75

FROM MODENA TO MARANELLO:
AFTER CARS,
MACHINE TOOLS

*One of the hydraulic grinders produced by Ferrari during the war.
Opposite, the trade-mark adopted for the machine-tools was Ferrari's Prancing Horse.*

After 1940 the Gran Premio Brescia della Mille Miglia was shelved. Regarding the 815 operation, one could not talk of success, but to call it a failure, as has been said and written by some people, would be too severe. Enzo Ferrari himself maintained in his book that the adventure did not have a happy ending, largely because of the haste in which the cars were built. On 10 June 1940 Italy entered the war. Ferrari and his colleagues, through problems deriving from the conflict, no longer found time to develop the 815, even less to think about racing. Consequently the 815's were put aside indefinitely.

"Years followed of experience that was very interesting if painful for me because cars were obviously out of the question" recorded Ferrari at the time. Because of the laws of industrial de-centralisation imposed on factories, Ferrari moved from Modena to Maranello in the last months of 1943, installing himself on some land he already owned. The firm changed from a joint-stock company to a private one, and in a short time it substantially increased in size. Whereas at Modena there had been about 40 workers, at

Maranello it soon rose to between 140 and 160 men. Initially Ferrari worked with diligence for the Compagnia Nazionale Aeronautica di Roma, until Enrico Nardi introduced him to Corrado Gatti, a machine tool dealer from Turin who persuaded the entrepreneur from Modena to work on the production of hydraulic grinders, a suggestion which Ferrari took up in order that his company could survive. This machinery, a product of Auto Avio Costruzioni, was embellished with the badge of the Prancing Horse.

Scuderia **Ferrari**

auto-avio costruzioni

Modena

"The end of the war did not find me unprepared, despite my workshops having been bombed on 4 November '44 and again the following February. I had always continued to make plans for racing cars, and when we got out of the storm I quickly got rid of the machine-tools." These words from Ferrari underline how the exciting experience of the 815 had not been forgotten.

In an article which appeared in the French magazine 'Fanauto', Maurice Sauzay, connoisseur of stories connected with the Cavallino, and in particular with the 815, declared, without wanting to upset the Ferrari 'appassionati', that objectively speaking this first attempt, more Fiat than Ferrari, did not lend great lustre either to the history of racing or to Ferrari.

However, Sauzay paid tribute to the ability of the technicians and mechanics who, were able to conceive, build and finish two examples of the car in time for its debut in racing in just four months. The real miracle, which was to be repeated habitually in the years that followed, started in 1946 when Ferrari officially became a constructor and could at last put his own name on all his cars, emblazoning them with the black Prancing Horse.

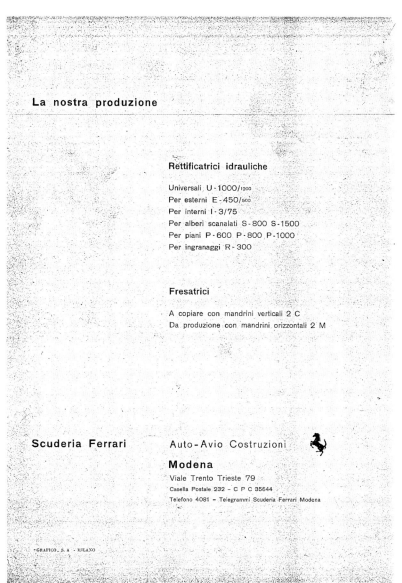

*Publicity brochure for the grinders built at Modena in Viale Trento e Trieste.*
*At the top of the page is a photograph of the two 815's, with the Prancing Horse.*

80    *The 'histories' of the two Auto Avio Costruzioni 815's in the official documents of the Public Automobile Registry.*

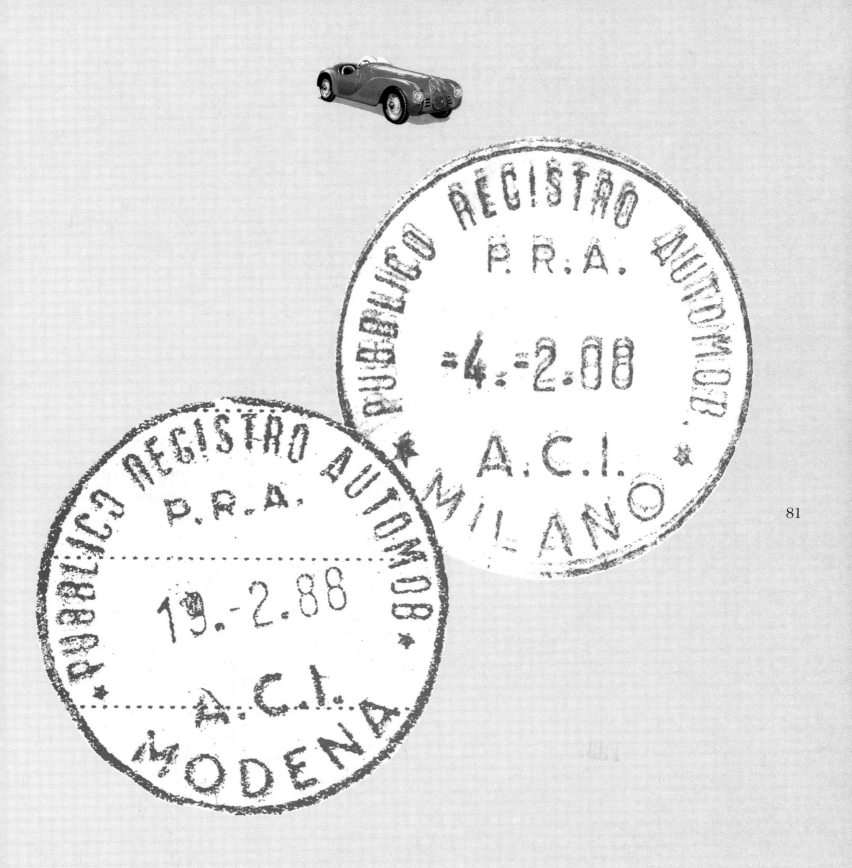

FROM OFFICIAL DOCUMENTS
THE TROUBLED HISTORY OF THE 815's

# VEHICLE SPECIFICATION

## LOTARIO RANGONI MACHIAVELLI

Car registration number MO 12539

| | |
|---|---|
| Date of registration: | 24th. April 1940 |
| Manufacturer | Auto Avio |
| | Costruzioni |
| Date of certificate of origin | 19 April 1940 |
| Engine number | 815/020 |
| Power | 21 bhp |
| Chassis no. | 815/020 |
| Type of body | Open |
| Purpose for which used | Private |
| Number of seats | 2 |

82

On 24 April 1940 Lotario Rangoni Machiavelli entered officially in possession of the 815 to participate in the Primo Gran Premio Brescia delle Mille Miglia.

After taking part in the race, the Marchese Rangoni left for the war and left the car with Ferrari for a complete overhaul. During the conflict, however, Rangoni died in a plane crash.

At the end of hostilities his brother, Rolando, tried to get the car running again. In the meantime Ferrari, preoccupied with the problems of machine tool production, had sent it back to Spilamberto, the Rangoni estate, as components in boxes. When the Marchese Rolando set to work on its restoration, he discovered that certain pieces were missing. The only way to complete the machine was to go back to Ferrari and ask for the

AUTOMOBILE CLUB D'ITALIA

UFFICIO DEL PUBBLICO REGISTRO AUTOMOBILISTICO

di *Modena*

IDENTIFICAZIONE E CARATTERISTICHE DELL'AUTOVEICOLO

N. della licenza di circolazione *28023 MO* — N. del motore *815-020*

Data del rilascio della licenza di circolazione: *28.8.52*

Potenza del motore in HP *21*

Fabbrica produttrice *Ferrari* — N. del telaio *815-020*

Data del certificato di origine *19.6.40* — Specie della carrozzeria *aperta* — Destinazione attuale *privato*

Tipo *815* — (eventualmente) Serie di fabbricazione — ALIMENTAZIONE *benzina*

Per le vetture ed autobus - Numero dei posti *2*

ISCRIZIONE DELLA PROPRIETÀ E TRASCRIZIONI
— già Targa 12539 MO —

---

missing pieces. "Ferrari told me he was sorry," said the Marchese, "but that he had had to give away all his automobile material because of the war."

The car was therefore put together with spare parts obtained from what sources were available.

Then, on 12 April 1947, by the terms of the inheritance, the car became the property of the deceased Lotario's heirs, who were his brother, his sister and his sister-in-law.

Following this Ferrari wanted to buy back the 815, and he got in contact with the Marchese Rolando Rangoni Machiavelli, who remembers: "He made me such a ridiculous offer that, in a quiet voice, I told him: "My dear Commendatore, when in the past I came to ask you for spare parts, you cut me off with hardly a word. Now you would like me to practically give you the car. I am sorry but I have no intention of giving you anything."

Following the loss of the number-plate, a new number was inscribed: it was MO 28023.

Rolando Rangoni Machiavelli maintains that the car finished in the hands of the car-breaker, who broke it up for spare parts. As at the present day, there no official document has been found which confirms the car's destruction ...

*Registration documents of the 815/020 belonging to Lotario Rangoni Machiavelli, initially registered as MO 12539 (on the opposite page), and after its change to MO 28023.*

## VEHICLE SPECIFICATION

**ALBERTO ASCARI**

Car registration no. MI 76356.

| | |
|---|---|
| Registration date | 25 April 1940 |
| Manufacturer | Auto Avio Costruzioni |
| Date of certificate of origin | 19 April 1940 |
| Engine no. | 815/021 |
| Power | 21 bhp |
| Chassis no. | 815/021 |
| Body-type | Torpedo |
| Purpose for which used | Private |
| Manufacturing series | 1940 |
| Number of seats | 2 |

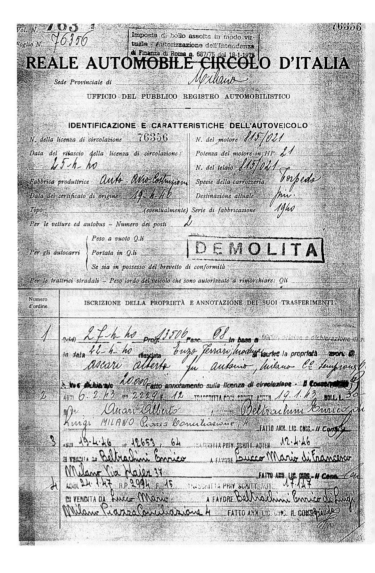

The official documents show that on 22 April 1940 Enzo Ferrari handed over the car to Alberto Ascari, who was living in Milan at corso Sempione 60. The actual cost of the car has never been known, but the declared price was 20,000 lire.

After the first G.P. Brescia delle Mille Miglia the fate of the car was rather mysterious. It is certain that Alberto never used it again, neither for racing nor for private motoring. One fine day in 1943, 6 February to be precise, Ascari sold the car to Enrico Beltrachini of Milan, living in Piazza Conciliazione 4, who acquired the 815 on deferred payments for a total of 42,000 lire. At the Public Vehicle Registry a legal mortgage was thus entered, cancelled later on 22 July 1943. On 19 April 1946 Beltrachini sold the car to Mario Lucco of Milan, residing at via Hayez 37.

After only nine months, on 24 January 1947, Beltrachini re-acquired the car from Lucco because, as a car enthusiast, he wanted to take part in some races. He reconditoned the 815 and made his debut on 11 May 1947 on the Piacenza circuit, interestingly enough at the same time as the first car to bear the name of Enzo Ferrari.

In that race Beltrachini retired on the tenth lap, a fate shared by the Ferrari of Franco Cortese. Still with the 815 he raced on the Vercelli circuit (1 June 1947), the only race which saw him reach the finishing line: fourth in the over 1,100cc class. Two more retirements were recorded with the same car at Vigevano (15 June) and Pescara (15 August) and from that moment, as far as racing was

*The official document released by R.A.C.I. (Reale Automobile Circolo d'Italia) shows the troubled history of Alberto Ascari's 815/021.*

concerned, the 815 was pensioned off. Beltrachini decided to sell it. On 7 November 1947 the car became the property of Alessandro Casiraghi, via Giocosa 15, Milan.

On 22 June 1948, the reason is not known, Casiraghi's property was confiscated. His debts amounted to 10,000,000 lire plus 500,000 lire in legal costs. Among the property seized from Casiraghi there was the 815.

On 26 February 1951, a document of the auction sale was issued from the court of Milan in which it appears that the 815 was allotted to Luciano Rossi of via Venini 50, Milan. On the same day the scrapping of the Auto Avio Costruzioni vehicle 815, registration MI 76356, was recorded. However, as far as we can tell, it was a 'demolition' that never happened. Having passed from one breaker to another, the car seems to have been taken

*The 815 in front of the entrance to the Autostrada dei Laghi, the first motorway in the world. Behind it is the wall bearing words celebrating the Fascist regime, signed by Mussolini.*

in by the enthusiastic organiser of a small, private museum near Modena. Peter Coltrin, a journalist and historian particularly close to the story of the Cavallino, identified the person in one of his writings on the 815 as Signor Emilio Fermi Storchi. He had acquired the car for a small sum and spent a little more restoring it, entrusting it to an expert repairer who however took a few liberties in restoring some of the missing parts. After a varied history Alberto Ascari's 815/021 finished in the hands of a well-known collector from Emilia.

The car was never shown to the public, and it probably cannot run by now. It reappeared only once, on the occasion of Ferrari Day, 18 September 1983. During this show it was exhibited in the courtyard of the factory at Maranello, open to the curious eyes of the many enthusiasts and experts who had gathered from all over the world. After that day of glory it disappeared once more.

LE AVTOSTRADE
SONO VNA GRAN
DIOSA ANTICIPA
ZIONE ITALIANA
E VN SEGNO
CERTISSIMO
DELLA NOSTRA
COSTRVTTIVA
POTENZA NON
INDEGNA DEGLI
ANTICHI FIGLI
DI ROMA
*Mussolini*

ROMA · XI · X
MCMXXV · IV

88 *The 815 photographed today. There is evidence that some liberties have been taken in its restoration.*

THE MYSTERY OF THE 815 ...
... WAS THERE A THIRD?

The history of the 815 is concluded with a collection of stories clouded by doubts and at times shrouded in mystery.

It appears that Alberto Ascari's 815 exists today: it is the property of a famous collector from Emilia. Strangely enough though, there is an official document which attests

# Nardi-Danes

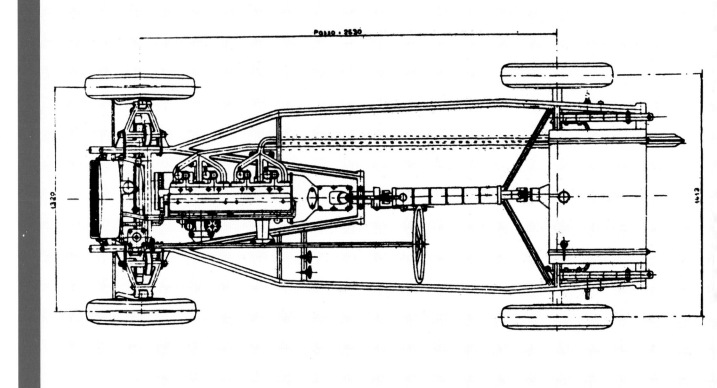

Passo - 2530

to the car having been scrapped. Of the other 815 on the other hand, which belonged to Lotario Rangoni Machiavelli, there is not a single trace left.

His brother, the Marchese Rolando, is sure that it was scrap-

91

*Technical drawing of the Nardi-Danese 1500 chassis with an in-line 8-cylinder engine, this appeared in a few races in 1947. With an engine apparently identical to the Ferrari 815, the Nardi-Danese 1500 was not successful.*

# 1500 - 1947

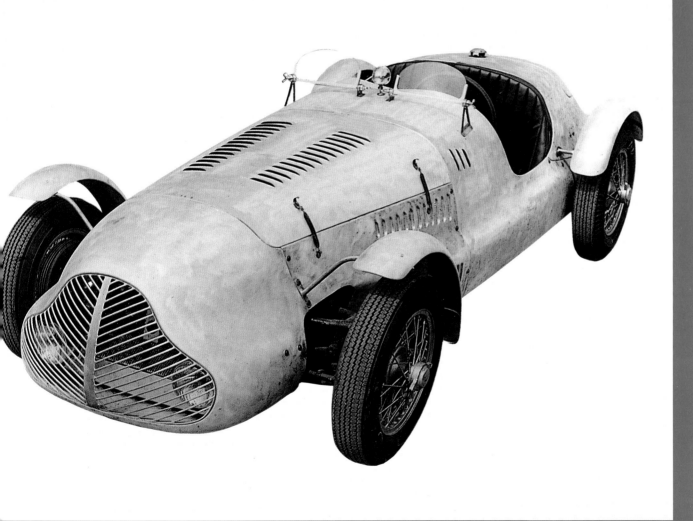

ped despite the lack of a document to prove it. There has always been someone who on various occasions has the existence of a third 815.

But it was always denied, especially by Enzo Ferrari.

Once the war was over, motor racing was taken up again in Italy. In 1947, when for the first time a car bearing the name of Enzo Ferrari entered the field, a few races saw on the starting line the 125 Ferrari (12-cylinder 1500) and the 815 Auto Avio Costruzioni (8-cylinder 1500).

At times another car would join them with a small plate on the bonnet bearing the name of Nardi.

When this car, at the technical check, opened its bonnet to be inspected it was noted that the engine was an in-line 8-cylinder 1500 identical to the 815 built at Modena, even if the body and chassis were different. No-one has been able to offer an explanation.

It is possible that the misunderstandings between Ferrari and Nardi at that time originated from the strange resemblance of the engine. However, both Ferrari and Nardi later preferred not to talk about that episode.

The destiny of the two 815's and the suppositions about the third are now surrounded in mystery, enigmas destined perhaps never to be explained.

A few black points in the brief and curious history of the 815, which came to be considered the forerunner, the 'anteprima', of all Enzo Ferrari's work.

*Two views of the in-line 8-cylinder engine fitted to the Nardi 1500. The initials ND are very evident on the tappet cover. Note the extraordinary similarity to the engine built at Modena for the 815's.*

*11 Agosto 1947, Circuito di Pescara. In prima fila, a sinistra, con il numero 21 la "125" Ferrari (1500 12 cilindri) di Franco Cortese la prima macchina a portare il nome del costruttore modenese; a destra, con il numero 23, la "815" Auto Avio Costruzioni (1550 8 cilindri) di Enrico Beltrachini.*
*L'unica foto che ritrae insieme la "prima" e l'"anteprima".*

*11 August 1947, Pescara circuit. In the front row on the left with the number 21 is the Ferrari 125 (12-cylinder 1500) of Franco Cortese; it was the first car to bear the name of Ferrari.*
*On the right, number 23, is the 815 Auto Avio Costruzioni (8-cylinder 1500) of Enrico Beltrachini. This is the only photo showing the 'Prima' and the 'Anteprima' together.*

AUTHOR
AND PLANNER
OF THE WORK:

**FRANCO VARISCO**

*Art direction and design:*
**Dario Bresciani**
**Renzo dell'Ungaro**

*English language editor:*
**Nicholas Dixey**

*Editorial co-ordination:*
**Daniela Zacconi**

*Photocomposition:*
**Studio Tabloid sas - Milan**

*Photolitho and printing:*
**Punto Grafico S.p.A. - Brescia, Italy**

*Copyright:*
**HYDE PARK GROUP plc, April 1990**
**ISBN 1-872718-01-9**

*Assistance from:*
**Carlo Montanaro**
**Gino Rancati**
**Alberto Redaelli**
**Daniela Zacconi**

*Photographs:*
**Andrea Fumagalli**
**Corrado Millanta**
**Franco Zagari**

*Illustrations and diagrams:*
**Attilio Cairati**
**Gianni Cavara**

*In addition, our thanks to:*
**Tonino Ascari**
**Gianni Bellentani**
**Giovanni and Mimmo Beretta**
**Carlo Felice Bianchi Anderloni**
**Dario Campagna**
**Pepi Cereda**
**Nicola Cutrera**
**Franco Gozzi**
**Christina Marina Maria Antonietta Minozzi**
**Roberta Nardi**
**Vittorio Palazzani**
**Rolando Rangoni Machiavelli**
**Antonella Scampini**
**Sandra Verdelli**

96